W9-ARA-303

Memoirs of War, 1914–15

CONTENTS

To Seymour Fink

MARC BLOCH

Memoirs of War, 1914-15

TRANSLATED AND WITH
AN INTRODUCTION BY
CAROLE FINK

Cornell University Press
ITHACA AND LONDON

ILLUSTRATIONS

Illustrations

ACKNOWLEDGMENTS

When, in May 1974, I discovered the *Souvenirs de guerre, 1914–1915* in the public library in Carpentras (Vaucluse), I could not imagine that the task of translation, and the research for its introduction, would bring such memorable, generous assistance as I subsequently received. Foremost was the help and encouragement of Étienne Bloch, oldest son of Marc Bloch, who provided personal documents, patient counsel, and wise insight into questions raised by the book. Fernand Braudel was exceedingly gracious in providing access to important documentation, as were Maurice Aymard, of the Maison de Sciences de l'Homme, Paris; General Porret, head of the Service Historique at Vincennes; the staff of the Bibliothèque de Documentation Internationale Contemporaine, Nanterre; and Rachelle Moore, of the State University of New York at Binghamton Library.

I should like to express my deepest thanks to Marilyn Rose of the State University of New York at Binghamton and to Marjorie Madigan of Manhattan-Marymount College for their wholehearted support and acute criticism. I

Acknowledgments

gratefully acknowledge the work of Professor Edward Fox of Cornell University, who made many valuable suggestions to improve the translation. The research for this book was aided by grants from the Inter-University Center for European Studies, Montreal, and the Research Office of the State University of New York at Binghamton.

The illustrations on pages 33, 50, 63, 82–83, 132, and 170–71 are reproduced courtesy of Étienne Bloch, Versailles, France. Those on pages 95, 100, 104, 106, 107, 113, 114, 116, 117, 118, 121, 123, 143, 145, 147, 148, 151, 158, and 160 are reproduced courtesy of the Musée des Deux Guerres Mondiales, Bibliothèque de Documentation Internationale Contemporaine, Université de Paris, Nanterre. The illustrations on pages 112, 139, 153, and 155 are reproduced courtesy of the Ministère de la Défense, État-Major de l'Armée de Terre, Archives Historiques, Vincennes. The map on page 86 was executed by Diane J. DePaso.

CAROLE FINK

Wilmington, North Carolina

Memoirs of War, 1914–15

INTRODUCTION

Marc Bloch and World War I

> I have served in two wars. I began
> the first, in August 1914, as an
> infantry sergeant.
>
> *L'étrange défaite*, p. 23

The impact of World War I on our contemporary culture remains a matter of controversy. "Modernism" had appeared before 1914 in all disciplines—in the arts, the humanities, the social and physical sciences. The prewar environment, bursting with world-imperialist expansion, technological innovation, intellectual and social ferment, had produced powerful and original works that broke through traditional ideas and methodologies. Yet the Great War itself constitutes an extremely important episode in the intellectual history of the twentieth century.[1] Immediately it became the great subject of poetry and lit-

---

[1] "It is not in the nature of war to create new ideas or new modes of expression. But the very situation of war itself was a new situation, in which the calamitous novelty was unprecedented in scale and impact" (Arthur Marwick, *War and Social Change in the Twentieth Century* [London, 1974], p. 84). Attempts to assess the impact of the Great War: Arnold Hauser, *The Social History of Art* (New York, n.d.), vol. 4; Hans Kohn, "The Crisis of European Thought and Culture," in *World War I: A Turning Point in Modern History*, ed. Jack J. Roth (New York, 1968), pp. 25–46; Paul Fussell, *The Great War and Modern Memory* (New York, 1975); and John U. Nef, *War and Human Progress* (Cambridge, Mass., 1950).

erature, of film and drama, of history and psychology, as well as the stimulus and model for medicine, engineering, and science. No other human episode has produced so large a literature of personal involvement—diaries, memoirs, letters, autobiographies, autobiographical novels, paintings, music. Scholars refer to a generation that, though it had come of age before 1914, was affected in varying degrees by the "wound of war."[2]

Writings on World War I continue to appear. Those that relate the experience of a historian possess exceptional importance, since such documents represent both a highly sophisticated temporal sensibility and a comprehension of larger, more profound forces. In 1969 the *Souvenirs de guerre* of French medievalist and economic historian Marc Bloch was published in Paris. It is a short work, essentially a fragment when compared with Bloch's *L'étrange défaite*, his powerful memoir and analysis of the fall of France in 1940. What makes the *Souvenirs* important, aside from the revelations of Bloch's first experience under fire, is that here we have a rare glimpse of a young, brilliant scholar destined to show heroism in two world wars and to die a martyr's death in 1944 before a German firing squad as a leader of the French Resistance. In World War I Bloch not only acquired the technical proficiency and leadership training of a soldier; here he renewed or reinforced his values and beliefs.

The *Souvenirs de guerre, 1914–1915* could stand alone, as an astute personal study of one sector during the first six months of war in France. Yet, after completing the translation, I felt it important to reconstruct Bloch's career over

[2]The phrase is in H. Stuart Hughes, *The Obstructed Path* (New York, 1966), p. 2.

the entire war: throughout the rest of his life he was to identify himself as a *poilu* and World War I officer.[3] Using his letters, private papers, and war journal, I started out to describe the nature of Bloch's 1914–18 military service. That undertaking led in turn to the still larger question of how Bloch's life and thought may have been altered by his war experience: how a gifted and mature intellectual, already a participant in important prewar struggles of French politics and historical scholarship, would subsequently give witness to the profound impact of World War I.[4]

Marc Bloch was born on July 7, 1886, in Lyons. His parents, Sara Ebstein Bloch (1858–1941) and Gustave Bloch (1848–1923) were French Jews. His paternal line originated in eastern France, where a great-grandfather, Gabriel (born in Metz in 1770 to a merchant family), fought in the French army against Prussia in 1793. His grandfather, Marc (born in Winzenheim in 1816), was an *instituteur public* in Strasbourg. His father, Gustave (born in Feyersheim, near Strasbourg), who had studied ancient history at the École Normale Supérieure in Paris and at the Écoles Françaises of Athens and Rome, fought in defense of Strasbourg in 1870. Emigrating in the wake of the Prussian annexation of

[3] G. I. Brătianu, "Un savant et un soldat: Marc Bloch (1886–1944)," *Revue historique du sud-est européen* 23 (1946): 16.

[4] No biography of Marc Bloch has yet been published. His papers are still in private hands, except for a collection at the École Normale Supérieure. Still, scholars disagree on whether Bloch's intellectual formation was substantially complete before World War I (Lucien Febvre, Preface to Bloch's "Critique historique et critique du témoignage," *Annales: Économies, sociétés, civilisations* [hereafter cited as *AESC*] 5, no. 1 [1950]: 1), was markedly altered by the conflict (Carlo Ginsburg, Preface to Marc Bloch, *I re taumaturghi* [Turin, 1973], pp. xi–xix), or did not reach full development until the mid-1920s (Bryce Lyon, Foreword to *French Rural History* [Berkeley, 1966], p. xii).

Alsace, Gustave Bloch received his first teaching position in the Faculty of Letters of the University of Lyons. In 1878 he married a twenty-year-old *lyonnaise*. Nine years later, a year after the birth of their second son, Marc Léopold Benjamin, the family moved to Paris, where Gustave Bloch had been appointed *maître de conférences* at the École Normale Supérieure; in 1904 he was named professor of Roman history at the Sorbonne.[5]

Marc Bloch grew up in a metropolis renowned as an intellectual and artistic capital, then gradually recovering from the defeat and civil war of 1870–71. The university reforms of 1877 brought an infusion of creative, Paris-trained thinkers back from the provinces—such men as Alphonse Aulard, Émile Durkeim, Charles Seignobos, Henri Bergson, and Gustave Bloch. A first generation of pioneering scholars was in the process of transforming historical instruction and research, not only to free them from German domination and salve the national pride but also to disseminate a liberal-republican spirit to French society.[6] The advances achieved by the new positivist and scientific methodologies, the increasing number of critical historical monographs and reviews, of courses and students, must have provided an exhilarating influence on the family of a gifted historian.

Gustave Bloch was a significant intellectual guide for his son Marc; Louis, the older brother, turned to science

[5]Genealogical information has been kindly supplied by Étienne Bloch, the oldest son of Marc Bloch. On Gustave Bloch (author of *La république romaine* [1913] and *L'empire romaine* [1922]), see the biography by J. Carcopino: *Association amicale de secours des anciens élèves de l'École Normale Supérieure, Annuaire de 1925*, pp. 86–109.

[6]William R. Keylor, *Academy and Community: The Foundation of the French Historical Profession* (Cambridge, Mass., 1975), pp. 391–92.

and medicine. Bloch *père* was remembered by a *normalien* as a "powerful instructor, terrifying yet affable," who taught Roman history with éclat.[7] Many years later Bloch recalled his father's pride in having possessed an adolescent "Strasbourg romanticism"—a quality that had long disappeared in Paris. His father's role as his first teacher and critic was acknowledged in two of Bloch's books.[8]

From 1894, when the Jewish General Staff officer Captain Alfred Dreyfus was first convicted of treason, to 1906, when he was finally exonerated of the false charges, the Dreyfus Affair shook the French intellectual community. Marc Bloch's generation had barely come of age during the crisis, but its political outlook was marked by the outcome.[9] Later in his life, Bloch placed himself at the end of a "short generation," distant from both the 1870–71 humiliation and the post-1906 reaction. He and his contemporaries had more in common with their republican, idealistic elders (from whose sway they were expected to liberate themselves, and did) than with the group that came along just one year later. Bloch's group inhabited the precatastrophe world of the *fin de siècle*—of enlightenment, liberal republicanism, patriotism with a measure of cosmopolitanism, scientific rationalism with a zest for so-

[7] Lucien Febvre, "Marc Bloch et Strasbourg: Souvenirs d'une grande histoire," *Combats pour l'histoire* (Paris, 1953), pp. 391–92.

[8] "À mon père, son élève," dedication of *Rois et serfs* (Paris, 1920), and Foreword 28 December 1923 (where Bloch expresses grief over his father's death), *Les rois thaumaturges*, new ed. (Paris, 1961), pp. vi–vii. March Bloch's mother's role as confidant and sharer in his projects is less well documented, but the flyleaf of *Apologie pour l'histoire*, according to his manuscript of May 10, 1941, was to read: "In memoriam matris amicae."

[9] Marc Bloch, *Apologie pour l'histoire ou métier d'historien*, 7th ed. (Paris, 1974) (hereafter cited as *Apologie*), p. 151. This work has been published in English as *The Historian's Craft*, trans. Peter Putnam (New York, 1953).

cial reform. Having witnessed a bitter national struggle that had been resolved by truth, it did not find its confidence shattered (as did many of its immediate followers) by the aftermath of the Dreyfus Affair: by alienation, social conflict, or a sense of discontinuity.[10]

In 1900, at age fourteen, Marc Bloch entered the ancient and distinguished Lycée Louis-le-Grand, where for the next four years he studied French, Latin, Greek, and English, along with chemistry and natural sciences. In 1904 he entered the elite École Normale Supérieure, which had just recently been incorporated into the University of Paris. Here Bloch worked with the leading French scholars and began his first historical research. He also attended lectures at the Sorbonne, the Collège de France, and the École Pratique des Hautes Études. At the École Normale, Bloch made many lifelong friends. From September 26, 1905, to September 18, 1906, he interrupted his studies for the obligatory military service, which he performed in the 46th regiment at Fontainebleau. After passing the *agrégation* at the École Normale in history and geography in 1908, he spent a year in Germany, studying under Karl Bücher in Leipzig and under Adolf von Harnack in Berlin. On his return to Paris in 1909, he received a fellowship from the Fondation Thiers which enabled him to devote the next three years to research on his doctoral thesis.[11]

[10]On the "1890–1904" normaliens: Robert Smith, "L'atmosphère politique à l'École Normale Supérieure à la fin du XIXe siècle," *Revue d'histoire moderne et contemporaine* 20 (1973): 253ff; on the "generation of 1905": H. Stuart Hughes, *Consciousness and Society: The Reorientation of European Social Thought, 1890–1930* (New York, 1958), pp. 337–44.

[11]Bloch on his teachers: "Christian Pfister (1858–1933): Ses oeuvres," *Revue historique* 172 (1933): 563–70; homage to Lucien Gallois in *L'île-de-France* (Paris, 1913), reprinted in *Mélanges historiques (Paris, 1963)* (hereafter cited as *MH*), vol. 2, p. 703, n. 1 (published in English as *The Ile-de-*

Introduction

Like many young republican scholars of the time, Marc Bloch was deeply influenced by the geographer Vidal de la Blache. [12] In Bloch's first investigations into medieval history, he chose to concentrate on rural history and specifically on the countryside around Paris. At the École Normale he had examined the landholdings south of Paris belonging to the chapter of Notre Dame. In his student writings he had already demonstrated a mastery of paleography and textual criticism and a keen imagination, which enabled him to link legal, monetary, religious, and archaeological evidence in a coherent rural history. In his formal recommendation to the Fondation Thiers, Bloch's mentor, Christian Pfister, wrote that his student was engaged in aspects of social history that had been neglected since the death of Foustel de Coulanges and which were currently dominated by German scholars. [13]

Marc Bloch's doctoral thesis was to be an investigation into the process of the eradication of serfdom in the regions surrounding Paris. It was clearly an effort to apply Vidal's teachings both on the impact of environment on human history and on the process of adaptation to natural

France: The Country around Paris, trans. J. E. Anderson [Ithaca, N.Y., 1971]) Ferdinand Lot, *Annales d'histoire économique et sociale* (hereafter cited as *AHES*) 6 (1934): 252–60 and 10 (1938): 61–63; "Charles-Victor Langlois," *AHES* 1 (1929): 583–84, and "Karl Bücher," *AHES* 4 (1932): 65–66.

[12]Marc Bloch, review of Lucien Febvre et al., *La terre et l'évolution humaine: Introduction géographique à l'histoire* (Paris, 1922), in *Revue historique* 145 (1924): 236. Geography as a "republican" discipline is discussed in Hughes, *Obstructed Path,* pp. 23ff.

[13]Christian Pfister to Fondation Thiers, Paris, April 29, 1908, Bloch–Febvre Correspondence, property of Fernand Braudel (whose permission is gratefully acknowledged), Archives Nationales microfilm (hereafter cited as AN) 318 MI 1; copies of Bloch's applications, May 1, 1908, and March 27, 1909, in ibid.

and material conditions. But, as he indicated in his fellowship statements, Bloch was also profoundly influenced by
Durkheim's sociology: he sought to draw comparisons
with the history of manumission in other regions of France
and to extract theoretical conclusions on the relationship
of liberation to land use in the thirteenth century, to
the development of a money economy, and to basic
changes in demography, law, literature, and religious
practice.[14]

During the period of the fellowship and research, Bloch
became connected with philosopher-historian Henri Berr's
new journal, the *Revue de synthèse historique*. This periodi-
cal represented both a revolt against fact-based academic
history and an answer to the challenge of sociology. It
attempted to introduce a theoretical, social-science ap-
proach into research.[15] Marc Bloch published several reviews in this journal, including his 1912 extended article,
"L'île-de-France."[16]

Marc Bloch's first published study, in 1911, displayed his
emerging themes and techniques.[17] It began with an
anonymous late-fourteenth-century chronicler's assertion
that 130 years earlier Queen Blanche, moved by the unjust

[14] Annual reports (1910, 1911, 1912) to Fondation Thiers, in ibid.
"[Durkheim] taught us to analyze more deeply, to come to grips with
problems more closely, and to think . . . less derivatively" (*Apologie*, p.
27).

[15] Martin Siegel, "Henri Berr's *Revue de synthèse historique*," *History
and Theory* 9 (1970): 328–34. Berr's 1900 manifesto, in the first issue,
translated by Deborah Roberts, is reprinted in *The Varieties of History*,
ed. Fritz Stern (New York, 1956), pp. 250–55.

[16] A fairly complete bibliography of Bloch's works, organized
chronologically, may be found in *MH*, vol. 2, pp. 1032–1104.

[17] "Blanche de Castille et les serfs du chapître de Paris," *Mémoires de la
société de l'histoire de Paris et de l'Ile-de-France* 38 (1911): 224–72, reprinted
in *MH*, vol. 1, pp. 462–90.

imprisonment of the serfs of the canon of Notre Dame, had the prison broken open and the serfs freed. Bloch presented a trenchant, frequently ironic reconstruction of the facts of the case: it was likely that the queen's overly ardent supporters misconstrued her pacifist purposes when they forced their way into the church; as the sovereign; she could simply have ordered the doors opened![18] Bloch then proceeded to demonstrate how the misreported incident provided the critical historian with evidence of *deeper realities* of the time: of the rivalry between church and state, centered on fiscal and juridical control of the serfs; of the incidence of rural revolt, focused on the arbitrary *taille,* and the seigneurs' counterreaction; of both the normal processes and variations of manumission; and, finally, of the expanding role of the Paris bourgeoisie in the countryside. Bloch had developed a two-tier methodology, consisting of demystification and critical social and political analysis. He was attempting to combine the scientific positivism of his historian-contemporaries with the new quest for synthesis.[19]

A second prewar article by Bloch[20] used a common

[18] "The compiler of the Grandes Chroniques [also] attributed the enfranchisement of the serfs of Orly to the intervention of Queen Blanche. . . . But his zeal as an official historian this time went too far. When the men of Orly were 'liberated from the yoke of servitude and mortmain,' the body of Blanche of Castille had been lying in the Abbey of Maubuisson for some eleven years" (*MH*, vol. 1, p. 490).

[19] This methodology is more fully developed in *Les rois thaumaturges.* Ginsburg (Preface, pp. xiv–xv) describes it as Bloch's effort to reconcile the "erudite probity of Langlois and Seignobos [who represented positivist historiography] with the problematic amplitude of Durkheim."

[20] "Les formes de la rupture de l'hommage dans l'ancien droit féodal," *Nouvelle revue historique de droit français et étranger* 36 (1912): 141–77; reprinted in *MH*, vol. 1, pp. 189–210.

though obscure medieval practice, the rupture of the feudal bond, as a springboard for an inquiry into historical reality. A twelfth-century text narrated the revolt of the vassals of Guillaume Cliton, count of Flanders, who was accused of violating his feudal obligations. Bloch's ostensible purpose was to clarify the exact procedure (the splitting or the throwing of the straw: *la rupture ou le jet d'un fétu*), whereby individuals could renounce their vassalage (or lords their seigneurial rights). Thus free, they were able to take the customary bellicose measures to "adjudicate" their grievances. For Bloch, this widespread ritual served as valuable evidence of the decline of feudalism and its ad hoc legal system and the subsequent revival of Roman law. He examined French, Flemish, and German chronicles, biographies, poetry, philosophical and legal texts. Bloch's characteristic style was to state the problem, present relevant texts, discuss possible (including patently erroneous as well as subtly false) solutions, and then come to a final resolution, allowing the remaining ambiguities and unsolvable questions to remain open. Although tolerant of the "legendary interpellations" of a twelfth-century copyist and of chroniclers too lazy to recount the most common practices, he was harsh with a German contemporary who constructed "picturesque analogies" from evidence carelessly analyzed.[21]

L'île-de-France: Les pays autour de Paris,[22] originally published in the *Revue de synthèse historique,* appeared as a book in 1913 in the series "Les régions de le France." Bloch admitted it was a preliminary description and that the re-

---

[21]Ibid., pp. 194–95, and Appendix: "La théorie de M. von Moeller [author of *Die Rechtsitte des Stabsbrechens*] sur la rôle de la rupture du bâton dans le droit médiéval," pp. 207–9.

[22]Reprinted in *MH*, vol. 2, 692–790.

gion's unity was based more on an "administrative misin-
terpretation" than on any historical, legal, or geographical
reality. In tones of passionate detachment characteristic of
a young predissertation scholar, Bloch scolded mendacious
chroniclers and well-intentioned but careless local historians. He grimly noted the history of errors, mediated
between contemporary theories, and pointed out work
that needed to be pursued—in meteorology, for example.
The book demonstrated his virtuosity in the use of linguis-
tics, geology, and geography, and in the use of evidence
from archeology, architecture, and folklore. It is a vivid
work, anticipating *Les caractères originaux de l'histoire rurale
française* (1931). It asserts Bloch's lifetime creed, that the
writing of history is an ungoing *process* of constructing the
reality of the past.[23]

Bloch's rural history did not single out individuals. Its
psychology was derived from a conception of the collective mentality and its interactions with the human and
physical environment.[24] Here he departed from his older
contemporary and later collaborator Lucien Febvre, who,
also exploring the terrain of collective psychology, concen-
trated on prominent individuals rather than attempting
rigorously to synthesize the characteristics of "peasants"

[23] "Every historical work worthy of the name ought to include a chapter, or, if one prefers, a series of paragraphs inserted at turning points
in the development, which might almost be entitled 'How can I know
what I am about to say?'" (*Apologie*, pp. 67–68).

[24] Bloch was influenced by Seignobos (*La méthode historique appliqué
aux sciences sociales* [Paris, 1901]) on the psychodynamics of historical
actors: "Since the historian of medieval labor history . . . does not see a
single worker or a single tool of the Middle Ages, he operates only on
the images that these things represent in his mind, and he represents
them only by analogy with the workers and the implements of the
present world that he knows to be analogous" (quoted in Keylor,
Academy and Community, p. 182).

or "petits bourgeois," the "authentic" inhabitants of historic regions.[25] Already in 1906, reflecting on history during his period of military service, Bloch had disputed the supposed dichotomy between the individual psyche and sociohistorical reality: "Society is but an ensemble of individuals... Its laws are superimposed over individual laws." In this mélange of realism and idealism, Bloch saw no dissipation of the individual in the mass. The task of the critical social historian lay in "psychosociology," in employing the most scientific methodological tools, such as philology and economics. Yet, as a *normalien* and an admirer of Jean Jaurès, Bloch also imbibed the antihierarchical, antideterminist bias of his classmates: he did not venerate Marxism (or Freudianism) and would always insist that the complex reality of human life was based on a "multiplicity of factors."[26]

In *L'île-de-France* Bloch demonstrated his treatment of "causes," a blend of subconscious, social, and material factors:

> The origins of Gothic architecture are still somewhat veiled in mystery.... One fact appears certain: wherever it was that saw the first vaulted transept of pointed arches, strong but light, supporting an arched roof, it was very probably not far from Paris and no doubt on the borders between the region of Paris and Picardy that the Gothic church arose and developed. It was there that the masons who did not dare to throw simple Romanesque arches across a rather wide space perhaps invented—or at any rate used more methodically than anyone before them—a most clever device: the

[25] Marc Bloch, review of Lucien Febvre, *Histoire de la Franche Comté* (Paris, 1912), *Revue de synthèse historique* 28 (1914): 356.

[26] Marc Bloch's journal (1906), seen with the permission of Étienne Bloch, and more fully developed in *Apologie*, pp. 121–29.

ogival vault; this, together with two other architectural con-trivances that followed it—the flying buttress and the pointed equilateral arch—are the marks of the new archi-tecture that we call Gothic. ... The new style spread rapidly throughout the Ile-de-France, whose solid lime-stone, which when quarried is covered with a resistant skin, tempted its master builders to indulge in great feats of daring. [*Mélanges historiques*, vol. 2, p. 767][27]

In 1912 Bloch began his teaching career, first as a profes-sor of history and geography at the Lycée in Montpellier, the next year at Amiens. On July 13, 1914, on the occasion of the distribution of prizes at Amiens, he delivered an ad-dress that summed up his historical ethos. He compared the historian to a "frail, blind physician," dependent on his "laboratory assistant" (the texts) to convey information to him, and also to a judge, who, charged with a vast inquiry into the past, gathers "testimony" from witnesses. "Historical criticism" was the "art of discerning from these reports the true, the false, and the probable."[28]

Bloch's exhortation to the students was partially au-tobiographical. He remarked on the shortcomings of memory ("a mirror blemished with opaque spots ... de-forming the images it reflects") and of the intellect ("like a basket with holes" which, in motion, drops parts of the memories it has gathered and, standing still, takes in only "extraordinary occurrences").[29] How could the historian—and the citizen—attempt to arrive at the truth?

[27] Bloch's interpretation of the interrelationship between technologi-cal development and the *mentalité* of an age is brilliantly developed in "Avènement et conquête du moulin à eau," *AHES*, 7 (1935): 538–63.

[28] *Critique historique et critique du témoignage* (Amiens, 1914), reprinted in *AESC* 5 (1950): 1–8.

[29] See pp. 77 and 89.

Only through habitual application of criticism to all testimony. No document became fact without a double process of scrutiny—of the object and of the observer.[30]

The reigning manual of historical practice was Langlois
and Seignobos's *Introduction aux études historiques* (1898),
which in Book 2, Chapter 7 ("Critique interne negative de
sincerité et d'exactitude"), systematically treated the problem of historical criticism. It had expressed optimism at the
prospects of banishing falsification from history.[31] Marc
Bloch had come to realize that falsification—whether
originating in crude ideological bias,[32] human error,[33] or
lack of methodological sophistication[34]—was inevitable,
and indeed a process itself worthy of study. That his own
generation had uncovered the Dreyfus forgeries, had con-
signed medieval legends to the disciplines of literature and
philosophy, and had created scientific standards for historical analysis was no guarantee against the recurrence of
wartime rumors. The outbreak of world war would give
profound proofs for Bloch's skepticism.

Finally, a study of Marc Bloch's thought before 1914 must
consider his already well-developed ideas of French patriotism. His father's 1913 study, *La république romaine*, emphasized as one of the causes of the destruction of Roman
democracy the growing turbulence and servility of the
masses—"without restraint, or dignity, or even, one

[30]Journal (1906) and *Critique*, in *AESC* 5 (1950): 2.

[31]English edition: *Introduction to the Study of History*, trans. G. G.
Berry (London, 1898), pp. 155–90.

[32]Marc Bloch, review of G. von Below, *Der deutsche Staat des Mittel-
alters* (Leipzig, 1914), *Revue historique* 128 (1918): 347.

[33]"Cerny ou Serin," *Annales de la société historique et archéologique du
Gâtinais* 30 (1912): 157–60.

[34]Review of Michel Augé-Laribé, *L'évolution de la France agricole*
(Paris, n.d.), *Revue de synthèse historique* 27 (1913): 167.

might say, without a *patrie*."[35] Marc Bloch, like many republican and especially Jewish scholars of his generation, viewed the history of France as a process in which the advancement of liberty and the formation of the French nation were intertwined. He, for example, considered the history of "provincial patriotisms... their grandeur and their decadence" as an "indispensable introduction" to the history of French patriotism. Bloch assumed the priority of studying the "ethnic unity" of the French people over burrowing in the details of the territorial formation of the French state.[36] In this he consciously opposed German historiography (and may have reacted to the impressions of his 1908–1909 sojourn in the Reich of Wilhelm II and Bülow, during the eruptions of the *Daily Telegraph* affair and the Bosnian crisis), which proclaimed that "the state is all, and the nation is of minor importance."[37] Bloch viewed the state merely as a vehicle, an inclusive rather than exclusive concept; he saw his role as citizen to be that of the *homme disponible,* comparable to the alert patriots of Republican Rome or the medieval representatives of French chivalry: a good Frenchman and a good European.[38]

Marc Bloch has just turned twenty-eight when World War I began. On July 31, during his holidays in Switzerland with his older brother, Louis, he learned of Germany's declaration of a state of war with France's ally, Russia. Arriving in Paris, at the Gare de Lyon, he learned

[35] Gustave Bloch, *La république romaine* (Paris, 1913), p. 168.

[36] *Revue de synthèse historique* 28 (1914): 356 and 365.

[37] *Revue historique* 128 (1918): 347, and, later, "Un tempérament: Georg von Below," *AHES* 3 (1931): 558.

[38] Smith, "L'atmosphère politique," p. 267, and Marc Bloch, *L'étrange défaite: Témoignage écrit en 1940* (Paris, 1957), which has been published in English as *Strange Defeat,* trans. Gerard Hopkins (New York, 1968).

of the assassination of Jean Jaurès. Despite widespread fears of civil disorders, Bloch noted the survival of the Socialist leader's noble spirit. The French people, inspired by his militantly republican idealism—by his vision of the "citizen soldier" and of the immense resources that the nation could draw on to defend itself against a stronger invader—almost unanimously flocked to the colors.[39] Like most of his compatriots, Marc Bloch was exhilarated by the national mood during the first days of mobilization: Paris was "quiet and somewhat solemn." The drop in motor traffic when busses disappeared and taxis grew scarce made the streets almost silent. Bloch observed both the "sadness" and the aura of "democratic fervor." There were only two classes: the nobility, who were leaving, and those who were not.[40]

Marc Bloch began keeping a journal, a daily record of his activities that he maintained throughout the war.[41] Dur-

[39] Jaurès's writings and theories of the nation at arms were collected in *L'armée nouvelle* (Paris, 1916). Bloch's journal for 1916 began with a Jaurès quotation: "The beauty of the profession of arms rests in its forcing man to be ready always to make . . . the supreme effort. There is nothing greater than . . . to give one's life, and I say this after thoughtful reflection, . . . for the homeland." Yet Jaurès's biographer Harvey Goldberg feels the chauvinism of the working classes to have been a betrayal of Jaurès's ideals: "With the speed of light, the ideal of international brotherhood crumbled before resurgent tribalism" (*The Life of Jean Jaurès* [Madison, Wis., 1962], p. 473). Bloch criticized the "Kienthal" mentality in *L'étrange défaite*, pp. 182–85.

[40] In vol. 2 of *La société féodale* Bloch explained France's cultural hegemony in the Middle Ages as having been based on its possession of "the most adventurous chivalry in Europe." See also Georges Altman ("Chabod"), Foreword to *L'étrange défaite*, characterizing Bloch's own *noblesse* in the World War II French underground.

[41] The journals are in the possession of Étienne Bloch, to whom I am grateful for an invaluable source. Not merely a record of places, people, and impressions, each also contains numerous personal notations: ex-

ing the spring of 1915, while recovering from a nearly fatal case of typhoid, he wrote the first part of the *Souvenirs de guerre, 1914–1915*. Here he recorded the "five amazing months"—August 1914 to January 1915—through which he had lived. In December 1916 or January 1917 while on temporary assignment in Algeria, Bloch wrote the second, unfinished part of the *Souvenirs,* a fragment describing his return to the front in June 1915.[42]

In order to reconstruct Bloch's experience, it has been necessary to seek out further evidence, especially since the journals kept later in the war contain but meager references to his activities. I have drawn on Bloch's private papers and letters,[43] the history of his regiments,[44] and his later writings that discuss the 1914–18 period, *L'étrange défaite* and *Apologie pour l'histoire.*

Germany declared war on France on August 3, 1914. On

---

penses, addresses, lists of books read, and important quotations. In 1917 we find a work plan for the thesis "Rois et serfs." A separate, undated notebook contains miscellaneous information: aerial photography (in which Bloch would be greatly interested after the war), lists and descriptions of topographic instruments, codes and signals, forms of the army's historical reports, and a questionnaire for prisoners.

[42] Part I of the *Souvenirs* is divided into six sections—from mobilization to the Marne; from victory to the trenches; trench warfare; combat in the Argonne; New Year's Day 1915; and reflections—altogether forty-five printed pages. Part II, consisting of four pages, is in one incomplete part.

[43] Bloch himself assembled a file, "Souvenirs de guerre," which included, along with his journals, documents covering the entire war period. This file, also in the possession of Étienne Bloch, is hereafter cited as File SG.

[44] "Le journal des marches" of the 272d and 72d regiments is housed in the Archives of the French Army, Vincennes (hereafter cited as "Journal des marches.").

August 4, the day of Jaurès's funeral, Bloch left Paris for
Amiens. He joined the 272d reserve infantry regiment
(18th company, 4th platoon) with the rank of sergeant,
which he had held since March 1907. On the official records he was described as almost 5 feet 5 inches, with brown
eyes and hair and an oval face. His photograph in uniform
shows a man of slight build and cultivated bearing, with a
neat mustache and unrimmed glasses. On August 10, at
1:30 A.M., his regiment left Amiens by train for the Meuse
region, near the Belgian border. En route he read his men
the news of the "capture of Mulhouse," perhaps at the
very moment that Bonneau's VII Corps had begun its
ten-mile withdrawal, ending the one-day liberation of Alsace.[45]

Bloch's regiment spent ten extremely quiet days in the
Meuse region. Except for presentiments aroused by the
"feverish atmosphere" nearby, this was a bucolic period:
calm, a little monotonous ("dozing on the grass"), amid
the spectacle of an "unknown countryside" not lacking in
charm. Then his regiment moved closer to the Belgian
border and was in proximity to what the men believed to
be a "great victorious battle," though on August 21 they
had learned that the Germans were in Brussels. Four days
later the retreat began, made more miserable by the
scorching heat, vast distances, dysentery, and sore feet,
not to mention the sad realization, for Bloch, of having
been mistaken.[46] The "brutal forced march" lasted seven

[45] The Germans had also just captured the Belgian fortress of Liège
(Barbara Tuchman, *The Guns of August* [Dell ed.; New York, 1971], pp.
213–14).

[46] Journals, August 25–September 5, 1914: Departures were usually at
4 A.M.; a twenty-five-kilometer march on August 29 ("unnerving in the

Marc Bloch in uniform, August 1914

33

days. Again, as in 1870, French troops witnessed the bitter
sight of peasants hastily evacuating their villages "before
an enemy against whom we could not protect them."[47]
The army stopped at the Marne.

For Marc Bloch's 272d regiment, the Battle of the Marne
took place on one day of intense fighting—September 10,
1914. Under a rain of bullets and shells, they advanced
only three or four kilometers from 10 A.M. to 6 P.M. and
sustained heavy casualties. In recalling this unforgettable
day some months later, Bloch expanded the terse description in his journal: he wrote of the sound and color of the
whirling and bursting shells and of the psychological reactions of men and officers under fire, as well as the noises
and smells of the battlefield at night when the combat had
ended. Describing the next morning, when the commanding brigade colonel passed on horseback and announced
the "victory," Bloch wrote:

> Despite so many painful sights, it does not seem to me that
> I was sad on that morning of September 11. Needless to
> say, I did not feel like laughing. I was serious, but my
> solemnity was without melancholy, as befitted a satisfied
> soul; and I believe that my comrades felt the same. I recall
> their faces, grave yet content. Content with what? Well,
> first content to be alive. It was not without a secret pleasure
> that I contemplated the large gash in my canteen, the three
> holes in my coat made by bullets that had not injured me,
> and my painful arm, which, on inspection, was still intact.
> On days after a great carnage . . . life appears sweet. Let
> those who will condemn this self-centered pleasure. Such

---

absence of news"); "sleeping in my pack, I dream of visiting Toledo"
(September 1); the first mail (September 5).

[47]Cf. a similar retreat in Emile Zola, *The Debacle, 1870–71*, trans.
Leonard Tancock (Penguin ed.; London, 1972), pp. 52–54.

feelings are all the more solidly rooted in individuals who are ordinarily only half aware of their existence. But our good humor had another, more noble source. The victory that the colonel had announced to us so briefly as he trotted by had elated me. Perhaps if I had thought about it, I might have felt some doubts. The Germans had retreated before us, but how did I know that they had not advanced elsewhere? Happily, my thoughts were vague. The lack of sleep, the exertions of the march and combat, and the strain of my emotions had tired my brain; but my sensations were vivid. I had little comprehension of the battle. It was the victory of the Marne, but I would not have known what to call it. What matter, it was victory. The bad luck that had weighed us down since the beginning of the campaign had been lifted. My heart beat with joy in our small, dry, devastated valley in Champagne.[48]

The French army pursued the Germans across the horrendous battlefield, past the sad vales of Champagne, littered with debris, corpses, and the remnants of the retreating army. Hot, thirsty, and tired, Bloch found consolation in the chase, but fell ill with fever.[49] By mid-September they had reached their farthest position—the Argonne Forest—and were quartered in the environs of Ste-Menehould. The weather suddenly grew cold. The men began constructing the first trenches in the forest of Hauzy. Bloch bitterly described how his men, poorly nourished and clothed, soaked by drenching rains and frozen during sleepless nights, blundered in their first

[48] On September 10 there were 593 casualties (including 54 officers killed or wounded) in a regiment of 2,021 soldiers and 171 officers (Ordre de Régiment, no. 2, September 11, 1914, "Journal des marches.").
[49] Journal, September 11–14, 1914.

35

constructions. The army's poor system of provisioning was observed with impatience.[50]

After Hauzy, they were quartered in La Neuville-au-Pont, a village Bloch came to know in intimate detail: its shallow river (the Aisne), railroad station, curved hilly streets, and especially the church on the main square:

> It was very old, its basic structure dating from the finest Gothic period. Its plan was simple, without a transept. The central nave was topped by two plain steeples, which rested firmly on the two aisles. The solid buttresses, which the master masons of the area had chosen over the lighter but more difficult flying buttress, provided the external support for the weight of the roof. Sober, robust, perhaps somewhat squat, it was definitely a country church. Yet it had some elegant features: its handsome Gothic western door and the north and south doors, where the Renaissance appeared.

The Neuville church was the scene of the frequent memorial services in which he participated on returning from the trenches. Weary soldiers crowded on the "massive wooden benches, beneath the modest nave and whitewashed arches." Bloch did not pretend that he found these experiences spiritually uplifting; he regarded them as the customary sad rituals of war.

Bloch found his first two weeks in the Argonne region nearly unendurable. Often the troops had to march, usually on short notice, into the countryside, to dig trenches

[50] Ibid., September 16–20 ("sojourn in the forest"), "Night and day, in a torrential rain, their feet in the mud, unable to defend themselves against the enemy's artillery, the officers and men displayed exceptional endurance" (Ordre, September 18, 1914, "Journal des marches.").

or fortify those already there. They never knew where they would sleep at night. The routine, although monotonous, was "not without danger." Mail finally arrived on September 26, but no newspapers were sold in Neuville and there were no books to read. September 29 was an "absurd day": an early rise, extensive trench digging under a brutal sun while an enemy plane hovered overhead. Suddenly shells exploded directly in the newly established trenches. While the men hurriedly withdrew, Bloch and the lieutenant searched under the rain of artillery shells for the wounded and for abandoned equipment. The sudden onset of twilight hindered their return to the regiment. Finally, Bonaffe, the battalion chief, rebuked the men for having abandoned their position.[51]

On October 1, "the first day of classes," Bloch was again in the Hauzy forest, where winter garments were finally distributed. The next cantonment was in Florent, a charming village whose huge trees were already tinted yellow and russet. It was situated between a forest to the north and a steep valley on the south. Bloch noticed in the homes the beautiful rustic furniture cut from the woods of the Argonne. The men washed and rested. During the night they dug trenches in the clearings under the direction of the corps of engineers. As an infantry sergeant, Bloch had almost nothing to do. He walked, rested, chatted with comrades, observed the nocturnal lights, and enjoyed the evening "silence," occasionally broken by the bursting of shells. The peaceful, rustic life, which re-

---

[51]Journal, September 29, 1914. The "Journal des marches" (September 29) records that the regiment was experimenting with a "new trench" divided into three parts, with shelters (*abris*) established on the outer wings; the center was to hold a minimum of six riflemen.

minded him of the late-summer days at the Meuse, ended abruptly when they left for the forest of La Gruerie.[52]

From October 1914 into January 1916, Bloch's regiment was employed in the forest of La Gruerie, defending a sector incessantly under attack by the armies of the German crown prince. The regimental history, which Bloch edited in 1917, summarized the period as follows:

> In addition to defending the sector, [the regiment] organized the area. It learned to manage tools, to use new equipment, and to apply itself to a new warfare—trench war, with its unceasing contest of mines, of grenades, and of trench mortars. . . . Despite all their attacks, despite their material superiority, the Germans made only insignificant gains: they never attained the route Vienne-le-Château/ Le-Four-de-Paris, which they tried so hard to reach. They did not pass.[53]

Warfare in La Gruerie was Marc Bloch's first experience of leadership in prolonged front-line combat. He was wounded there and received his first promotion. The troops entering the forest climbed a steep, winding path. The autumn weather had become icy. Each section took up its assigned position on the front line and stayed there except for an occasional period in the rear. At first there were no trenches, only "sharpshooters' foxholes . . . Our predecessors could hardly have blistered their hands on the handles of their shovels." The enemy was from forty to one hundred meters away. Nightfall brought the dread of surprise attack. Bloch recalled with chagrin six months later that on their first night in the front lines his section

---

[52] Journal, October 1 and 6.
[53] "Historique du 72ᵉ Régiment d'Infanterie, août 1914–1917," File SG.

had misinterpreted the Germans' routine nocturnal firing (a perfectly "harmless gesture") and responded with a "furious fusillade." They had foolishly sacrificed their rest, wasted scarce ammunition, and sprayed their poorly coordinated shots at peaceable people in the rear.

On October 18–19 Bloch's section underwent a brutal attack, and his leadership was recognized. His captain, telling Bloch's men they could confidently follow him under fire, called him a real *poilu*—because of his unkempt beard, Bloch felt sure.[54] The mark of a good officer was obvious: during an action, he had to "keep his head high," in full view of the men, to direct accurate firing, at the risk of being shot at himself—a danger of which Bloch was keenly aware.

The Gruerie experience made Bloch reflect on the nature of "courage":

> Not always, to be fair, but often it is the result of an effort . . . that a healthy individual makes without injury to himself and which rapidly becomes instinctive. . . . Death ceases to appear very terrible at the moment it seems close: it is this, ultimately, that explains courage. Most men dread going under fire, and especially returning to it. Once there, however, they no longer tremble. Also, I believe that few soldiers, except the most noble or intelligent, think of their country while conducting themselves bravely; they are much more often guided by a sense of personal honor, which is very strong when it is reinforced by the group.[55]

Bloch, who considered individual *noblesse* the essential component of collective acts of bravery, expressed openly

[54] Journal, October 19.
[55] Bloch again defined courage in *L'étrange défaite,* pp. 138–40.

the "profound disgust that the few cowards in [his] platoon inspired in [him]." The *Souvenirs de guerre* gives us portraits of officers who were both brave and sensitive to their men's needs along with those who treated the men brutally, hoarded provisions and news, and stayed behind in safe shelters.[56] Bloch also describes his companions, many of whom he lost to death and injury. Except for one sergeant, who managed a wineshop near the Bastille, all of his soldiers came from the countryside or from small French cities. The Bretons had great difficulty using the French language, once with dire consequences. The peasants and miners, brave and patriotic, had, observed Bloch, more difficulty supporting scenes of hideous death than he.

Bloch complained, as he would again twenty-five years later in *L'étrange défaite*, of the "total inadequacy" of their material preparations. At first there were no barbed wire, no heavy tools for trench construction, no telephone communication either between trenches or to summon artillery support from the rear.[57] In fact, there was a universal shortage of matériel in the entire French army in October 1914; the first month of fighting had consumed over half the total stockpile of ammunition. Progress came slowly. By December 1914 Bloch noted that new equipment was beginning to arrive in La Gruerie, the men had learned the techniques of construction, and the French artillery matched the uproar of the enemy cannon.

[56] See *L'étrange défaite*, pp. 141–42 (especially n. 1) and *passim*, for World War II.

[57] In order to "transmit orders . . . , to carry ammunition or supplies, we had to move in the open, exposed to the enemy's fire and often to his view." *L'étrange défaite* describes similar unpreparedness for *Blitzkrieg* (pp. 79ff and *passim*).

Introduction

In La Gruerie, with the perpetual whistling of bullets and the danger of an unseen enemy, skill in observation was crucial. Bloch remarked that because of his "weak vision," he always placed an accurate observer beside him during the day. At night, however, like one of his childhood James Fenimore Cooper heroes, he used his ears to analyze the sounds of the "great nocturnal murmur": "the tap-tap of the raindrops on the foliage, so like the rhythm of distant footsteps, the somewhat metallic scraping sound of the very dry leaves falling on the leaf-strewn forest floor (which our men often mistook for the click of an automatic loader introduced into a German rifle breech)."[58] Twenty-five years later he wrote:

> Ever since the Argonne in 1914, the buzzing sound of bullets has become stamped on the gray matter of my brain as on the wax of a phonograph record, a melody instantly recalled by simply pushing a button; too, even after twenty-one years, my ear still retains the ability to estimate by its sound the trajectory and probable target of a shell. [*L'étrange défaite*, p. 84][59]

Each tour in La Gruerie generally lasted about eight days, followed by a week in the "monotonous quiet of the camp." Bloch's second stay in the forest left a "pleasant memory," despite bloody episodes and his first exposure to gas. On his third tour, Bloch was promoted to adjutant, which meant better food and quarters, and access to news and to the society of officers. When he left La Gruerie, on

[58] Journal, October 14, 1914.

[59] Bloch is comparing his familiarity with shells with his (and the French army's) *inexperience* with aerial bombardment.

November 15, Bloch ceased to write in his journal. The *Souvenirs* was then based on "memories that have remained quite clear."[60]

When they returned to an icy forest on November 21, the trenches were better constructed. The forest was by now largely mowed down by barrages of shells and bullets. This time the Germans were only twelve meters away. The "most dangerous hours" occurred immediately after the regiment's arrival. After that, "live and let live" had to prevail between the neighboring trenches.[61] During this sojourn, Bloch was wounded in the face and the head. Calculating after the passage of the critical "first two minutes" that he would probably survive, he had his wounds treated in the rear and then returned at once to the front lines.

During the next rest, they occupied Vienne-le-Château, a village so close to the combat zone that it was shelled incessantly: "With its crumbling walls, its houses ripped apart . . . its smoking debris, and its steeple with the top blown off, it was Arras or Rheims in miniature." As an officer, Bloch was able to sleep in a room with a bed and enjoyed the infrequent staff meetings. There was pillaging and also a tragic cave-in of one of the soldiers' mud huts, in which three men died. In Vienne they learned of General Joffre's order for an offensive to "liberate the territory." The promised end to the slow, dreary, and dispiriting trench warfare was soon frustrated. The cannon roared, the enemy responded weakly, a violent battle

[60]Journal, November 15, 1914.
[61]A. E. Ashworth, "Sociology of Trench Warfare, 1914–1918," *British Journal of Sociology* 19 (December, 1968): 407–23, discusses the nonaggressive tactics of proximate enemies.

occurred on the other side of the Argonne. Then there was no further talk of an offensive.[62]

When they returned to the front lines in December, the French had inched their way to the edge of the forest, reaching the Servon–Vienne-le-Château road. Before them lay a vast horizon and the belfry of Binarville—a goal often mentioned in the soldiers' talk but never realized. The trenches were muddy in December. The rains were not absorbed by the clayish, defoliated terrain. There was the unceasing work of bailing and reconstruction and the constant discomfort of muddy clothes and tools. On January 3, 1915, at the beginning of another tour in the trenches, Bloch asked authorization to return to quarters. He had been stricken with typhoid fever.

During Bloch's first "five astonishing months" of warfare, he had gained many insights. Once mail began arriving and he began receiving newspapers, he followed the debate between the French and Germans over the "Manifesto of the 95 German Intellectuals," which had been signed by many prominent historians.[63] Bloch also observed the myopia and closed-mindedness that caused the army to block promotions to noncommissioned officers who, though brave, lacked "connections." In the expectation of a short war, the military made no "needful pruning operations" or urgent promotions.[64] Later he would learn of the epidemic of false rumors that had erupted at the

[62]"Captain Q." (Pierre Quentin-Bauchart, a historian who died at the Somme), informed Bloch of the Joffre offensive, and quoted the order in his *Lettres Août 1914–Octobre 1916* (Paris, 1918), p. 45. See also Jean Bernier's novel *La Percée* (Paris, 1920).

[63]"Souvenirs de guerre—première période," File SG.

[64]*L'étrange défaite*, p. 143.

start of the war—of the French airplane that allegedly bombed Nuremberg, the Belgian *francs-tireurs*, German atrocities, and the legendary Russian landings in August 1914 in Scotland and Marseilles. While such manufactured news as "the hanging of Antwerp priests [upside down] as living clappers to the bells that rang the German victory of October 1914[65] had little impact on the men in the trenches, that environment produced its share of *fausses nouvelles:* lack of regular news from outside, the closeness of the enemy, the frequent reliance on mouth-to-mouth communication made inaccuracies quite common.[66]

On June 1, 1915, having recovered from his illness, Marc Bloch wrote his will.[67] He distributed his money to war charities and to students of the École Normale, his books to friends and to his family. He specified his desire for a "purely civilian funeral." In an accompanying letter to his sister-in-law, Marie, he expressed sadness at the prospect of death but also deep satisfaction that he had not fallen, like those of August 1914, during the retreat, "while still in despair for France." Now he felt "sure of victory and happy . . . to give his blood for it."[68] It has been estimated

---

[65]The story of ringing church bells in the *Kölnische Zeitung* became transmuted via reports in *Le Matin, The Times,* the *Corriere della Sera,* and *Le Matin* into an atrocity/heroism tale (Robert Graves, *Goodbye to All That,* 2d ed. rev. [Garden City, N.Y., 1957], pp. 67–68).

[66]Marc Bloch, "Réflexions d'un historien sur les fausses nouvelles de la guerre," *Revue de synthèse historique* 33 (1921): 48–52; and *Apologie,* pp. 89–90, 94–95.

[67]Paris, June 1, 1915, "Voici mes dernières volontés . . ." Seen by permission of Étienne Bloch.

[68]Marc Bloch to Marie Bloch, June 1, 1915. Cf. Bloch's "Testament spirituel," Clermont-Ferrand, March 18, 1941, published in *Annales d'histoire sociale* (hereafter cited as *AHS*), 1945: "Hommages à Marc Bloch," translated in *Strange Defeat,* pp. 177–78.

that during the first five months of World War I, one of
every three French combatants was killed or wounded.
Casualties in August alone were close to 300,000.[69] Marc
Bloch was proud of having shared the agony and survived, of having returned immediately and voluntarily to
the front. He later explained that his "military spirit"
emanated from the tradition of loyalty of his French-
Jewish ancestors and also from a republican's sense of
"virtue."[70]

On June 5, 1915, Bloch ended his convalescent leave and
went to the army depot at Morlaix to await assignment. He
found the life of a garrison town dull and dispiriting.
Good men who, "once thrown into the furnace," com-
ported themselves with honor became a crowd with weak
hearts performing mean and base actions, who panicked
at the anticipation of distant danger. Burning "to be useful," Bloch volunteered for service with the 72d regiment.
His parents and sister-in-law came for a sober farewell.
The train ride back to the front is described colorfully in
the second part of the *Souvenirs de guerre:* the view of a
peaceful countryside and of the bustling industrial town of
Creusot. There was one dramatic episode, involving a bul-
lying stationmaster at Is-sur-Tille.

Bloch had no idea where his journey would lead: was
the 72d in Alsace, in Artois, or at the Dardanelles? He
ruefully discovered that he was returning to the Argonne
and would remain there for more than a year, until 1916.
Headquarters were in the pleasant village of Les Islettes, a
large and prosperous town spread out on the Paris–

[69] Tuchman, *Guns of August,* p. 488.
[70] *L'étrange défaite,* pp. 23–25 and 221–22.

Verdun route, surrounded by fields and woods, its houses and barns filled with troops. Until the battle of Verdun, a year later, this was a sheltered location. The enemy had not yet installed the long-range batteries that could strike the peaceful village.

Bloch saw action shortly after his arrival. On July 13 the enemy launched a heavy attack all along the Argonne front with a prolonged bombardment accompanied by gas.[71] There were no further major engagements that summer. The "defensive" war of attrition resumed. The summer heat was stifling. Bloch was again wounded on August 2, apparently not seriously. He received his first citation in the regimental order of August 7 for his intelligent leadership and for demonstrating the "greatest bravery in the face of danger."[72]

For the remainder of 1915 Bloch's journal provides only the briefest itineraries, with an occasional meteorological notation. On September 23–24, at Claon, he noted Joffre's proclamation of still another great offensive. Fifty-four French and thirteen English divisions, supported by 1,500 pieces of artillery, launched an offensive in Champagne along a front of almost ninety kilometers. The army in the Argonne was to divert the Germans from the main thrust of the attack, which was finally halted on October 13. The headlong, violent actions of 1914–15, aimed at a breakthrough, gradually gave way to the controlled, continuous, and equally costly offensives of 1916.[73]

[71]Journal, July 13–15, 1915; "Historique du 72ᵉ Régiment d'Infanterie," File SG.

[72]Journal, August 2, 1915; Ordre du régiment, August 7, 1915, copy in File SG.

[73]Cyril Falls, *The Great War, 1914–1918*, Capricorn ed. (New York, 1961), p. 116.

Bloch was still in the Argonne at the start of the year. His journal begins with a quotation from Jaurès: the duty of an officer was to master himself, to maintain "lucidity" in command, to retain it even in the face of death; a sort of "sublime ambiguity" must be maintained as to which side of death one stood on.[74]

In January 1916, during Bloch's first extended leave in Paris, the first German Zeppelin raid on the French capital took the lives of twenty-four people. Paris was also beginning to experience material privations. Some *poilus* returned from their leaves indignant at the "normality" of civilian life and at the inflamed (often manipulated) chauvinism of the civilians. By contrast, except for the boorish stationmaster, Bloch did not resent the "home front." Indeed, he later discerned that reactionary forces would exploit the front soldiers' resentment and invent civilian scapegoats and *Dolchstoss* legends as excuses for poor military leadership and, eventually, for coups d'état. Bloch acknowledged that there was a "real rear" in World War I where, but for the occasional accident, there were unravaged fields and peaceful, often prosperous towns in whose cafés the war simply meant verbal arguments over strategy. His response was characteristic: "Crouching in the trenches, we trembled for the safety of our families."[75]

The 72d was one of the few French regiments that did not participate in the defense of Verdun when the German attack began in February 1916. Remaining on the other side of the Meuse, they were nonetheless under extremely heavy bombardment. On the night of March 24–25 Bloch

[74]Journal, 1916, quoting from *L'armée nouvelle*.
[75]*L'étrange défaite*, pp. 167–68. On the home front: Gabriel Perreux, *La vie quotidienne des civils en France pendant la Grande Guerre* (Paris, 1966).

led a detachment of grenadiers on a mission to distract the Germans from an attack on their trenches. He received another citation for this action on April 3, and a day later was promoted to second lieutenant.[76] On April 9 he recorded in his journal that he had had to spend two hours inside a shelter because of the heavy shelling.[77]

In August 1916 Bloch's regiment prepared to join the Joffre offensive at the Somme. First they were kept in reserve, but by the beginning of October they were in the front lines at the recently recaptured Bouchavesnes. There, weary and with inadequate shelter, they withstood the powerful German counterattack on October 14–15.[78] Shortly afterward, this costly and only partially successful Somme offensive was halted. Like the German failure at Verdun and the all-too-successful though impermanent Russian breakthrough in the Carpathians, it would have momentous political repercussions. Civilian populations, experiencing the privations of the harsh 1916 winter, clamored for victory. The emerging leaders of the combatants (soon including the United States) aimed not for a negotiated end to the slaughter, or even for increased

[76]Ordre de la Division, April 3, 1916, File SG. The promotion, listed as temporary "by ministerial decision," was made permanent a year later, on April 3, 1917 (Registre Matricule du Recrutement, vol. 9 [1907], no. 4277, Archives of the French Army at Vincennes).

[77]Journal, 1916: heavy bombardments (March 19–20), patrol (March 23–25), "unnerving bombardment" (March 26–28), "spring" (March 29), front lines (April 4–9). On April 10 Bloch revisited La Harazée, and on April 18 Ste-Menehould. On Easter Sunday, April 23, 1916, he was back at the front.

[78]Journal, October 5–13; "Historique du 72ᵉ Régiment d'Infanterie," File SG.

cooperation among the allies, but for national triumphs that would both redeem the suffering and cement their regimes.[79]

A new field of action awaited Marc Bloch. After two more brief leaves in Paris, he was sent with his regiment on December 14, 1916, to Algeria. They were assigned there to restore order in the Sahara, where an insurrection had followed closely upon draft disorders in a number of North African cities.[80] Bloch's stay, which included assignments in Philippeville, Constantine, Biskra, and Algiers, was seemingly uneventful. The regiment returned to France in late March, and Bloch again went to Paris.

In May he was sent to make advance arrangements for the regiment's new position west of St-Quentin, adjacent to the English sector. The spring weather was pleasant, and activity was limited to patrols.[81] In the meantime, the Nivelle offensive had been repulsed by the Germans at the Chemin des Dames. The French army had mutinied. Henri-Philippe Pétain took command on May 15 and began instituting reforms. Bloch's regiment was then ordered into the area near the Chemin des Dames. From June 21 through July 2 it participated in the "brutal battle of the observation posts" in the valley of Cerny-en-Laonnois. Twice they were attacked by barrages of

---

[79]Arno J. Mayer, *Wilson vs. Lenin: Political Origins of the New Diplomacy, 1917–1918* (New York, 1964), pp. 141–90. Cf. Winston Churchill, *The World Crisis, 1916–1918* (London, 1927), pp. 171–96.

[80]Journal, December 15, 1916–March 27, 1917; André Nouschi, *La naissance du nationalisme algérien* (Paris, 1962), p. 25; and Claude Martin, *Histoire de l'Algérie Française* (Paris, 1963), p. 257.

[81]Journal, May 12–14, 18–19, 26–28, 1917.

Bloch (middle, rear) with fellow noncommissioned officers in Algeria,
December 1916

Minenwerfer as heavy as those thrown against them at the Somme.[82]

The summer brought another quiet period. On September 7, back near the Chemin des Dames, a German reservist from Bremen was captured. In their excitement the cooks confused "Brème" with "Braisne" (a small French village to the north), and rumors flew that the prisoner, in peacetime a wholesale merchant, had been a spy living in France before the war. Bloch later used this incident to illustrate the processes that produced the ubiquitous wartime rumors.[83]

Marc Bloch was now assigned to the regimental command post as an intelligence officer. He described his duties to his closest friend, the sociologist Georges Davy, as "topography, observation, information about the enemy, and a series of minor functions customary to staff headquarters, such as rendering into good French the proposals for citations."[84] Bloch's new position gave him more leisure to read, to plan his future career, and also to think about the war.[85] To Davy he confided his fatigue, his concern about his health, and a certain distractibility—a "discontinuity of intellectual effort"—which the war had

[82]"Rapport de M. le Lieutenant-Colonel, Commandant le 72ᵉ Régiment d'Infanterie sur les combats du 21 juin à 2 juillet" (in Bloch's hand: "redigé par moi"), File SG.

[83]Journal, September 7, 1917; "Réflexions d'un historien sur les fausses nouvelles de la guerre," pp. 53–57, repeated in *Apologie*, pp. 93–94. On September 8, 1914, because of an aural reversal relayed through official channels, Bloch's regiment had been misinformed of the Russians' capture of "Ber-lin," rather than their actual capture of "Lemberg" (cited in Quentin-Bauchart, *Lettres*, p. 222).

[84]Bloch to Georges Davy, September 16, 1917, AN 318 MI 1.

[85]Bloch's journal for 1917 contains a "plan" for his thesis and a list of books he had read.

intensified. Bloch had strong if mixed feelings about the past three years and about the conduct of the war, but not about its ultimate outcome. Victory would come, yet as a historian he knew that "great crises move slowly." He was dissatisfied with the bureaucratic orientation of the army, which had been formed under peacetime conditions, and with the "pseudo-historians" of the École de Guerre, who forgot that their profession was the "science of change." Unhappy with the wasteful rules of seniority that kept inferior career officers in command, Bloch had respect only for the men; in the face of their "heroic resignation," he felt "humble" with his intellectualized sense of acceptance.[86]

The regiment soon returned to combat, supporting Pétain's offensive at the Fort of Malmaison.[87] Bloch received his third decoration for having held his observation trench under heavy enemy shelling in order to obtain invaluable information for the command post.[88] Malmaison, a carefully planned, innovative action combining tanks, surprise, and coordination of armies, gained for the French the heights of the Aisne. It also increased their self-confidence. In November 1917 Clemenceau returned to power with promises of vanquishing Germany. In the

---

[86]"Since all these humble persons, who do not have the same source of strength as we, resign themselves heroically, truly it would be dishonorable not to do as well as they, if not better" (Bloch to Davy, September 16). Also, Marc Bloch to Louis Bloch, November 27, 1917, in the collection of Étienne Bloch.

[87]"Historique du 72e Régiment d'Infanterie," Ordre no. 128 (secret), Bloch's *mémoire* describing reconnaissance missions, November 2–3, File SG.

[88]Ordre de la division, November 17, 1917: "Excellent intelligence officer. During the recent October operations he maintained the division's observation service with ability, consistent energy, and remarkable courage" (AN 318 MI 1).

same month, Émile Durkheim died and was mourned by one of his colleagues as "another casualty of the war."[89]

During the last year of fighting, the exhausted French army underwent the Wagnerian finale to over four years of bloodshed. With Russia out of the war, Ludendorff tried to effect a gigantic breakthrough in the west by launching five successive attacks, using storm troops and gas. The German army reached within fifty-six miles of Paris, which they began to shell with an extraordinary long-range gun. Bloch's duties during the final twelve months of the war grew more diverse. His war file contains résumés of reliefs and the occupation of enemy trenches, an outline of political and economic subjects, a model questionnaire, and his notes on the interrogation of French deserters (whom he defended before the Conseil de Guerre). There are also captured German propaganda documents, reports on leave policy, and signals and codes used in liaison between the services and between the allies. He was also reading extensively and wrote for the *Revue historique*.[90]

In June 1918 the 72d regiment was in the Forest of Retz when the Germans launched their fourth offensive against the French front on the Aisne. After the attack, Bloch received another citation for his bravery under fire: in a zone under heavy bombardment, he had made a number of dangerous reconnaissance missions, providing his chief with intelligence that was crucial to the success of the operation.[91] A month later, before Villemontoire, the 72d joined the costly assault, which was also the beginning of the German retreat. Bloch's journal records the German

[89] Gustave Bloch to Georges Davy, November 17, 1917, ibid.
[90] Gustave Bloch to Davy, January 27, 1918, ibid.
[91] Ordre de la Division, no. 116, July 16, 1918, ibid.

departure (August 2) and the final pursuit—by truck, but more often on foot—toward the east. On August 18 he was promoted to the rank of captain. On September 16 they had reached Nancy, where, ill, he had a brief leave. The chase continued through a cold, rainy autumn. Shells rained on their positions (November 1). The roads were clogged with trucks (November 7). The ancient battlefields they now crossed were "desolate" (November 8). After the armistice,[92] they resumed their march to the Rhine. The journal ends with their arrival, on November 30, 1918, at Neuf Brisach in Alsace.

Bloch remained in the army until May 13, 1919. From January 21 until his discharge, he was attached to the Ministry of Security for Alsace and Lorraine, stationed in Strasbourg as an intelligence officer.[93] Upon returning to his parents' home, at 118 avenue d'Orléans in Paris, he resumed civilian life and also prepared for his marriage, on July 21, to Simone Vidal. His fiancée, daughter of an *inspecteur général des ponts et chaussées* (who during the war had been responsible for both the navigation of the Seine and the provisioning of Paris by water), was the descen-

[92]Bloch saved *Le Journal* of November 12, 1918 ("1,561st day of the war"): "Germany surrenders!" Bloch's journal for November 11 has only the notation "Armistice." File SG contains the text of Foch's announcement, signed by Mignon for the 72d regiment at 10 A.M. on November 11, 1918, announcing that the armistice would go into effect in one hour. Did Bloch draft this announcement?

[93]Charles-Edmond Perrin, "L'oeuvre historique de Marc Bloch," *Revue historique* 199 (1948): 163. Bloch's File SG contains a series of bulletins (December 5, 8, 12, 15, and 17, 1918) which he may have edited or to which he may have contributed, dealing with such subjects as the monetary transformation of Alsace and Lorraine, France's wartime agricultural production, postwar Franco-American collaboration, the reconstruction of agriculture in the liberated regions, and the great Rhine ports.

dant of a family of industrialists and engineers, related to the Dreyfuses. Simone Vidal, who herself was decorated for war service to prisoners and refugees, was to become her husband's secretary and close companion. They had six children.[94]

In October 1919 Bloch was named *maître de conférences* at the University of Strasbourg, newly reopened as a French institution and headed by his mentor, Christian Pfister.[95] Bloch would spend the next seventeen years in Strasbourg, as a member of a young, vibrant faculty that included historian Lucien Febvre and sociologists Charles Blondel and Maurice Halbwachs. With its central location and its vast library of medieval history, Strasbourg provided the resources and intellectual stimulation for Bloch's great period of teaching and writing.[96]

In 1920 Marc Bloch submitted an abbreviated version of his thesis, "Rois et serfs," to the Sorbonne. Where he had once planned to analyze the character of rural life throughout the Ile-de-France during the era of serfdom,

[94]Étienne Bloch, "Marc Bloch: Une vie complète" and "La ligne maternelle d'Étienne Bloch," both in AN 318 MI 1.

[95]Lucien Febvre, "Marc Bloch et Strasbourg: Souvenirs d'une grande histoire," Publications de la Faculté des Lettres de l'Université de Strasbourg, *Memorial des années 1939–1945* (Paris, 1947), pp. 171–82. On November 22, 1919, Pfister delivered an inaugural address in the presence of Raymond Poincaré, president of the Republic, and representatives of the army, the government, the church, and the French Institute, as well as numerous foreign scholars. He characterized the return of Alsace to France as the triumph of "right and justice." The text is printed in Henri Salomon, "Christian Pfister," *Revue historique* 172 (1933): 561–62.

[96]Febvre, "Marc Bloch et Strasbourg," pp. 181–82; G. Canguilhelm, "Maurice Halbwachs" [who died at Buchenwald], *Memorial des années 1939–1945*, p. 230. Following the pattern of the generation before them, many of the *strasbourgeois* returned to posts in Paris in the 1930s, including Febvre and Bloch.

he had to confine himself to one not insignificant detail: the manumission of serfs in specific locales by the last Capetian kings. Again a narrow case study served Bloch well. He was able to analyze key features of the political, social, religious, and legal climate of the thirteenth century through his investigation of two early-fourteenth-century documents. Despite the embellishments of later interpreters, Bloch proved that the warrior monarchs' collective enfranchisement of their serfs was no more than a means of enhancing the royal revenues.[97] Having completed his prewar obligation and established his professional credentials, Bloch, along with other members of his prematurely aged generation, moved rapidly into the leadership of French scholarship.

What impact did World War I have on Marc Bloch's life and thought? Such a question, in the absence of extensive personal documentation, is difficult to answer. Immediately after the war, like his beloved "master" and friend Henri Pirenne, Bloch returned to scholarly concerns that seemed remote from his own time.[98] With but a few exceptions, he did not use the analogy of 1914–18 (as did so many of his contemporaries) in his writing and teaching.[99]

[97]Marc Bloch, *Rois et serfs: Un chapître d'histoire Capetienne* (Paris, 1920). Bloch's notes for the thesis are in Box 53, "Thèse," in the Papiers Marc Bloch, Bibliothèque de l'École Normale Supérieure, Paris.

[98]Bryce Lyon, *Henri Pirenne: A Biographical and Intellectual Study* (Ghent, 1974) discusses the Pirenne-Bloch friendship.

[99]Interview with Marie-Thérèse d'Alverny, July 31, 1977 (Paris). In *Les caractères originaux de l'histoire rurale française* (Paris, 1931) Bloch refers to "villages . . . reconstructed piece by piece, as happened in our own day in zones devastated by the Great War." The article "Réflexions d'un historien sur les fausses nouvelles de la guerre" was Bloch's only published study of the war until the 1969 publication of *Souvenirs de guerre*.

According to his own testimony in *L'étrange défaite,* Bloch
devoted most of his time during the twenty postarmistice
years to his career and his family. Like their counterparts
in the United States in the years following World War II,
the former *poilus* and their noncommissioned officers
turned civic, moral, and military leadership over to older
and more reactionary individuals and institutions in ex-
change for *la bonne vie.* [100]

Yet it is inaccurate to describe Bloch as having totally
withdrawn from public affairs. Both as ex-combatant and
as a professional economic historian, he scrutinized the
German reparations question. He knew France's powerful
adversary, which had just barely been defeated, could and
would refuse to pay, and that the ancient, bloody quarrel
would, under even less favorable conditions, soon resume.
He blamed the Third Republic's "ineptitude": agreeing to
high though illusory figures, invoking sanctions, supporting the "dead horse" of Rhenish separatism, and, finally,
invading the Ruhr.

Though admitting the impossibility of anticipating the
Nazi revolution, Bloch later judged that France should
have encouraged the "still timid" liberal, pacifist forces of
the Weimar Republic, not antagonized Great Britain or fed
the resentments in Germany on which Hitler's movement
flourished. He castigated France's leaders for obscuring
the nation's war devastation and limited industrial poten-
tial behind the grandiloquence of Louis XIV in the early
1920s and, when faced with the inevitable German revival,
of seizing the gloomy defeatism of Louis XVIII. Though

---

[100]*L'étrange défaite,* p. 215: "I belong to a generation that has a bad
conscience." Cf. Bloch to Febvre, October 19, 1939, AN MI 318 1.

Bloch's work prevented him from remaining active in the military reserve (which also meant he was blocked from further promotions), he read the army literature thoroughly, especially on new offensive techniques. In *L'étrange défaite* he accused his fellow intellectuals, scientists, and social scientists, who were accustomed to dealing with "great impersonal forces," of undermining French democracy: "fearing the crowd's opposition, our friends' sarcasm, and the ignorant incomprehension of our leaders," working passively on electoral committees instead of leading political movements they were not "partisans." None risked becoming a voice in the wilderness. [101]

Bloch's public reaction to the war experience was his strong support of comparative history. He took over Pirenne's advocacy of a truly international discipline and unceasingly advocated—and practiced—scholarship free of parochialism and prejudices. [102] The founding, with Lucien Febvre, of the journal *Annales* in 1929 was a pathbreaking episode in the post-World War I environment. Bridging disciplines and time boundaries, the *Annales* was the fruition of Bloch's prewar aspirations toward exploration and synthesis and the expanding of the frontiers of his chosen discipline. It also expressed the postwar realization that historical reality transcended the context of a single nation, its ideology, its culture, and its writers. [103]

[101] *L'étrange défaite*, pp. 198 and 215–17; Bloch to Davy, March 28, 1921, AN 318 MI 1; "État Major—École Supérieure de la Guerre," Papiers Marc Bloch, École Normale Supérieure, Box 54.

[102] "Pour une histoire comparée des sociétés européenes," *Revue de synthèse historique* 46 (1928): 15–50.

[103] Maurice Aymard, "The *Annales* and French Historiography (1929–1972)," *Journal of European Economic History* 1 (1972): 492–97; also

Bloch also took an open stand against the chauvinism practiced by his fellow historians. Reacting against both such wartime manipulations of reality as the Manifesto of the 95 German Intellectuals of 1914 (signed by his German mentors) and postwar ultranationalism (as exemplified by H. G. Wells's grand design for a "universal history," which was tainted by a virulent francophobia),[104] Bloch set a living example of *Weltbürgertum*. He attended numerous international conferences. He mastered almost every major European language. He also undertook, for the most part alone, to write summaries of German historical scholarship for ten years in the *Revue historique,* from 1928 to 1938, essays that are models of both erudition and critical insight.

Marc Bloch returned to Paris in 1936 after a long wait for appointment to the Sorbonne. The city was in the midst of Popular Front ferment; the nation was as divided as during the Dreyfus Affair. This time, however, the French Right borrowed from a foreigner, Adolf Hitler, an alternative ideology to the *"république juive."* An influx of 70,000 East European Jewish refugees between 1919 and 1939, who clustered in a veritable ghetto in the fourth arrondissement, helped to stimulate an anti-Semitism already rising at the specter of Leon Blum's "social revolution."[105] The almost entirely assimilated French-Jewish community could not believe it was in danger. Bloch, who favored the

---

Hughes, *Obstructed Path,* pp. 38–39; Keylor, *Academy and Community,* p. 211; and Georg Iggers, *New Directions in European Historiography* (Middletown, Conn., 1975), pp. 56–79.

[104] "H. G. Wells, historien," *Revue de Paris* 4 (1922): 860–74.

[105] David Weinberg, *Les Juifs à Paris de 1933 à 1939* (Paris, 1974), pp. 15–20; also Henri Noguères, *La vie quotidienne en France au temps du Front Populaire, 1935–1938* (Paris, 1977).

Popular Front, knew how little the Jewish leadership, like
the Catholic hierarchy, supported revolutionary goals.[106]
Yet though a nonpracticing Jew, he was alert to the spread
of prejudice and to the use of the synagogue as scapegoat.
When the Popular Front fell in 1937, even the French Left
deserted the Jews. For Bloch the period had personal repercussions when, on the advice of Lucien Febvre, he felt
it prudent as a Jew to withdraw his candidacy for the
directorship of the École Normale Supérieure.[107]

Bloch shared the dream of French Jews in the liberaliz-
ing influence of education, which he had personally experienced in pre-World War I Paris. He devoted himself in
the 1920s to reforms in the teaching of history, in the 1930s
to curricular reform in French higher education, and during World War II to a "revolution" in education.[108] Bloch
encouraged his students to explore original research questions. They could draw on his broad background and his
trenchant criticism, but were never restrained by his
domination.[109] Bloch's and Febvre's hopes for new
methods of teaching were to some extent realized after
World War II in the founding of the Sixth Section of the
École Pratique des Hautes Études: an influential center of

[106]Étienne Bloch, "Marc Bloch," AN 318 MI 1.

[107]Febvre to Bloch, n.d.; Bloch to Febvre, December 7, 1938, both in
ibid.

[108]"Sur les programmes d'histoire de l'enseignement secondaire,"
Bulletin de la société des professeurs d'histoire, November 1921, pp. 15–17;
"Pour le renouveau de l'enseignement historique: Le problème de
l'agrégation" (with Lucien Febvre), AHES 9 (1937): 113–29; "Notes pour
une révolution de l'enseignement," *Cahiers politiques* 3 (August 1943).
Also *L'étrange défaite*, pp. 196–97.

[109]Robert Boutruche, "Marc Bloch vu par ses élèves," Publications de
la Faculté des Lettres de l'Université de Strasbourg, *Memorial des années
1939–1945*, pp. 195–207.

teaching, research, and publication with which France has assumed leadership in a truly internationalist scholarship in the social sciences.[110]

Opposing the ethos of French interwar military thought, Bloch remained a convinced Jaurèsian. The "victory" had been costly to France: almost a million and a half in dead alone and a staggering total of three million wounded. It had consumed billions of francs and left the northeastern regions ruined. The archaic system of French finances subverted the Republic's efforts toward restoration and security. The French army was convinced that the war had taught the efficacy of defense over offense, of the artillery over the infantry, of matériel over men. Marc Bloch drew the opposite conclusion. To him the real hero in the war was the *poilu,* whose courage and tenacity made the difference *despite* an impossible system of liaison, procurement, and supplies.

It was in this spirit that Bloch, although fifty-three years old and a veteran with six minor children, allowed himself to be called up in 1939. Knowing that he opposed the reigning official wisdom epitomized by the Maginot Line, he wrote to a student during the *drôle de guerre:* "A great psychological problem . . . a nation in arms that does not make war, . . . an army that is mobilized yet lacks all sense of danger. To be sure, I understand the meaning of the con-

---

[110]Aymard, "*Annales* and French Historiography," p. 503. The institution, recently separated from the University of Paris, has been renamed the École des Hautes Études en Sciences Sociales; it is located in the same building—the Maison de Sciences de l'Homme—as the journal *Annales*. In the spring of 1979, to commemorate the fiftieth anniversary of the *Annales*, the EHESS presented a memorial exhibition on the life and work of Marc Bloch.

cern for saving human life among those leaders who are dominated by the images of the hecatombs of 1914–17...."[111]

Bloch nevertheless invoked the noble spirit of the "most precious friendships" of his life, two men who had fallen in 1914: a miner from Pas-de-Calais and the manager of a bistro near the Bastille, both described in *Souvenirs de guerre.* He contrasted the enduring strength, good sense, courage, and patriotism of the *menu peuple*—the workers and the peasants—with the shortsightedness and ephemeral pretensions of the ruling classes.[112]

Bloch fought again, in the disastrous campaign of June 1940, which he analyzed that summer, as a combatant and mature historian, in *L'étrange défaite.* As a Jew, he was forced to leave German-occupied Paris and surrender his co-editorship of the *Annales.* He continued to write for the journal, however, under the pseudonym "Michel Fougères"; prepared a lengthy, posthumously published study of Europe during the barbarian invasions; and worked on his *Apologie pour l'histoire.* Settling in Vichy France, he refused to emigrate either to Algeria or to the Unted States, where he had received offers to teach, though he understood the dangers of remaining in Hitler's Europe. He became a professor at the University of Strasbourg-in-exile, at Clermont-Ferrand, then at Montpellier, where he became active in the Resistance. When the Nazis occupied all of France in 1942, Bloch, a delegate of the *franc-tireur* group of the MUR (*Mouvements Unis de Résistance*), moved to his birthplace, Lyons, where he became one of the leaders of the French underground. He

---

[111]Bloch to Philippe Wolff, January 4, 1940, quoted in Boutruche, "Marc Bloch vu par ses élèves," p. 105, n. 1.

[112]Bloch to Febvre, May 4, 1940, AN 318 MI 1. Also *L'étrange défaite, passim.*

Last photograph of Marc Bloch, ca. 1944

traveled extensively, even to Paris, and wrote for the Resistance press. He strongly favored the indigenous democratic organizations in France over the London-based government in exile.[113]

In the spring of 1944 Bloch was captured by the Germans, imprisoned in the fortress of Montluc, and tortured. On June 16, almost thirty years after Jaurès's assassination, Bloch—along with twenty-six young patriots—was shot by the Gestapo at St-Didier, near Lyons. His last words were "Vive la France."[114]

Bloch's experience in World War I undoubtedly influenced his writing of history. Yet since his opus is vast—as were the breadth of his interests and the scope of his erudition—we can only suggest, rather tentatively, areas in which the war changed his thought. Though Bloch himself resisted the limitations of *schématique*, it would be useful, given the question that inspired this introduction's first paragraph, to outline and analyze five important concepts: *mentalités*, historical reality, historical determinism, the *longue durée*, and the quest for synthesis.

Mentalités. In the spring of 1919, while still in the French army, Bloch confided to his fellow officer and future colleague Charles-Edmond Perrin that after the war he intended to study the consecration of the French monarchs

---

[113]On Bloch's career in the Resistance: Étienne Bloch, "Marc Bloch," AN 318 MI 1; Altman, Foreword to *L'étrange défaite*, pp. 7–18; and Henri Michel, Preface to Sauret edition of *L'étrange défaite* (Paris, 1973), p. 17.

[114]Charles-Edmond Perrin, "St. Didier de Formans," courtesy of Fernand Braudel, Maison de Sciences de l'Homme, Paris. Perrin was the only surviving witness to the scene. Shot by the Gestapo firing squad, he feigned a mortal wound and later escaped. Lucien Febvre had immediately instituted an inquiry: "Documents concernant la mort de Marc Bloch" (1944), AN 318 MI 1.

at Rheims.[115] He did not write on this subject afterward, but in the 1920s Bloch produced works of extraordinary originality on popular conceptions—and misconceptions— regarding kingship: *Les rois thaumaturges* (1924),[116] a study and critique of almost ten centuries of belief in the royal touch as a cure for scrofula; "La vie d'outre-tombe du Roi Solomon" (1925),[117] a brilliant inquiry, based on a multitude of sources, into Anglo-French legends of the profligate monarch's painful though not eternal sufferings in the vision of afterlife so central to medieval mythology; and "Saint Édouard le Confesseur" (1923),[118] a virtuoso exposé of the distortion of the life and works of England's "last national monarch" (who, in a papal election trade-off, was canonized a century after his death) by the enthusiasms and ambitions of the official hagiographers.

Bloch's concentration on the problem of popular false beliefs centered on monarchs is not fortuitous. Even earlier, before World War I, he must have experienced the iconoclasm of the librarian Lucien Herr at the École Normale Supérieure toward all three "sacred institutions"— church, army, and monarchy—whose allegedly mystic powers held the people in thrall.[119] After four years of

---

[115]Charles-Edmond Perrin, "Preface," *MH*, vol 1, p. xi.

[116]*Les rois thaumaturges: Étude sur le caractère surnaturel attribué à la puissance royale, particulièrement en France et en Angleterre* (Strasbourg, 1924; Paris, 1961), published in English as *The Royal Touch: Sacred Monarchy and Scrofula in England and France*, trans. J. E. Anderson (Montreal, 1973).

[117]*Revue belge de philologie et d'histoire* 4 (1925): 349–77, reprinted in *MH*, vol. 2, pp. 920–38.

[118]*Annalecta Bollandiana* 41 (1923): 5–131, reprinted in *MH*, vol. 2, pp. 948–1030.

[119]Smith, "L'atmosphère politique," p. 251. Cf. Bloch's "Pourquoi je suis républicain? Réponse d'un historien," *Cahiers politiques* 2 (July 1943): 9–11, dissociating the French monarchy with "great ideas," such

intense propaganda and censorship of news, of powerful images focused on warrior (or beneficent) monarchs, Bloch broke through in the 1920s with original and provocative studies of collective psychology.[120]

Bloch's "Réflexions d'un historien sur les fausses nouvelles de la guerre" (1922) emerged almost as an instinctive reaction to the war experience.[121] Here he systematically analyzed the material, social, and psychic conditions (of which the 1914–18 war was a prime example) of the ubiquitous false rumor in history. Although Bloch left this subject in the 1930s for other inquiries, the large place he accorded "fraud and error" in *Apologie pour l'histoire* (1941) proves its enduring importance to him. Twice he referred to an obvious contemporary forgery: the Protocols of the Elders of Zion. Bloch was doubtless aware of its impact both on the gullible and on the already convinced. He obliquely described the process of its dissemination during the interwar period and explained the ease with which it found a receptive audience among the deprived, the alienated, and the resentful. With his studies of falsehood, Bloch was a pioneer investigator of collective men-

---

as those that inspired and galvanized the French people in 1914–18. Significant, too, are the words of his father, Gustave Bloch (*L'empire romaine* [Paris, 1922], pp. 11–12): "The national tradition and the republican tradition are identical. One cannot be sacrificed without giving up the other."

[120] See Bloch's important reviews: of M. Halbwachs, *Les cadres sociaux de la mémoire* (Paris, 1925), in *Revue de synthèse historique* 40 (1925): 73–83; of Charles Blondel, *Introduction à la psychologie collective* (Paris, 1928), in *Revue historique* 160 (1929): 398–99; of Georges Lefebvre, *La grande peur de 1789* (Paris, 1932), *AHES* 5 (1933): 301–4; and of Johannes Spör, *Grundformen hochmittelalterlicher Geschichtsanschauung* (Munich, 1935), *AHS* 1 (1939): 105–6.

[121] Bloch to Davy, May 14, 1922, AN 318 MI 1.

talities, a field in which later practitioners—Febvre, Mandrou, Lebrun, Tenenti, and Vovelle—have continued to expand this moral vista of history.[122]

Historical reality. In 1941 Bloch wrote:

> Here in the present . . . is that vibrance of human life which only a great effort of the imagination can restore to the old texts. I have frequently read and have often narrated accounts of wars and battles. Did I truly know, in the full sense of that word, did I, before I myself had suffered the terrible, sickening reality, comprehend what it meant for an army to be encircled, what it meant for a people to be defeated? Before I myself had breathed the joy of victory in the summer of 1918 (and though, alas, its fragrance will never again be the same, I yearn to breathe it a second time) did I truly know all that was contained in that beautiful word?[123]

The historian "loved life," and, moreover, he "borrowed freely from his daily experiences . . . shading them, where necessary, with new tints." The historian's ability to name things—and to understand names—"would be quite meaningless if we had not known living people."[124] Bloch, like Pirenne and Febvre, paid homage to Jules Michelet, who before World War I had been all but banished by the "scientific" historians because of his "passion." Marc Bloch and Henri Pirenne prided themselves on the inseparability of history and life, both of which should be dedicated to advancing human values—

[122]Georges Duby, "Histoire des mentalités," *L'histoire et ses méthodes* (Paris, 1961), pp. 937-66.
[123]*Apologie*, p. 48.
[124]Ibid.

"intelligence, insight, intuition, realism, compassion, understanding," along with courage and love.[125]

After World War I, critical method became for Bloch a means and not the end of historical inquiry. While he continued to acknowledge his debts to Langlois and Seignobos, masters of technique who were products of a more serene era, Bloch and his contemporaries viewed their scholarly role anew. It was not sufficient simply to acquire methodological skills, or to gather and analyze data rigorously. The questions one asked were of equal, if not greater, significance.[126] The war had undoubtedly increased the historian's tools and expanded his critical consciousness; yet for Bloch the *act* of participation in the human suffering and triumph was indispensable to the practice of his craft.

Historical determinism. After World War I Bloch turned more firmly away from all determinist systems. "Homo economicus was a straw man, not only because he allegedly was preoccupied solely by self-interest; the worst illusion was to believe it were possible to form a clear conception of his self-interest. Napoleon once said: 'There is nothing so rare as a plan' . . . ."[127]

Bloch sought to disprove other "illusions," such as the "pseudo-necessities" of terrain—of rivers as secure boundaries and valleys as undefendable. The last war had belied both notions. Too, it has shaken faith in "technological progress," given the weight of resistance to change and the crucial human dimension of adaptation.[128]

[125] Lyon, *Henri Pirenne,* pp. 459–60 and *passim.*

[126] *Apologie,* p. 26. Also J. Stengers, "Marc Bloch et l'histoire," AESC 8 (1953): 336–37.

[127] *Apologie,* p. 158.

[128] Review of Lucien Febvre et al., *La terre et l'évolution humaine: Intro-*

Bloch was equally impatient with new forms of determinism: the fashionable *Geopolitik,* used to justify either the status quo or revisionism, but lacking an appropriate historical or ethnic validity.[129] In respectful though critical tones he also took issue with Friedrich Meinecke's 1936 work on "historicism":

> So many astonishing things . . . : this individualization, almost deification of the state, which has been instinctively elevated to the level of the most incontestable truths of evidence . . . ; this notion of a historical thought that seems to culminate between Goethe and Ranke, and . . . ceases to progress after them . . . ; this negation (despite a few cautionary and polite formulas) of all efforts undertaken during this century to integrate the understanding of particular events into a larger human science: assuredly still quite timid efforts and somewhat uncertain, but of which no one has the right to say in advance that they will be fruitless, or worse, that they lack elegance; finally and above all the pretentiousness to have uncovered *"l'esprit"* of a science while at the same time refusing absolutely to discuss the development of its techniques . . .[130]

"Human facts," Bloch stated, "are in essence psycholog-

---

duction *géographique à l'histoire* (Paris, 1922), *Revue historique* 145 (1924): 235–40; "Technique et évolution sociale," *Revue de synthèse historique* 41 (1926): 91–99; response to Lefebvre des Noëttes in *Revue de synthèse historique* 43 (1927): 87–91; "Les 'inventions' médiévales," *AHES* 7 (1935): 235–40; "Technique et évolution sociale," *Revue de synthèse historique* 41 *Europe* 47 (1938): 23–32; and especially "Avènement et conquête du moulin à eau," *AHES* 7 (1935): 538–63.

[129] "Géographie et politique," *Revue de synthèse historique* 56 (1936): 267–68; also "Un problème de contact social: La colonisation allemande en Pologne," *AHES* 6 (1934): 593–98, and *Apologie,* pp. 125–26.

[130] "'Historisme' ou travail d'historiens?," *AHS* 1 (1939): 429–30.

ical facts."[131] Bloch, who displayed brilliance in searching out the meaning of words and symbols, legends and false rumors, knew all too well that the act of "linkage" itself is critical: "A civilization, like a human being, cannot be assembled mechanically like a puzzle. A grasp of details that have been studied completely separately... will never produce knowledge of the whole; indeed [this procedure] will not achieve an understanding even of the pieces themselves."[132]

The longue durée. After the war, Bloch hesitated before finally returning to his studies of the peasants and the countryside. In the process, he drove himself to "perfect his erudition" in all the areas relating to rural history, which culminated in his 1929 Oslo lectures and the publication, in 1931, of *Les caractères originaux de l'histoire rurale française.* His book, which revolutionized the study of agrarian history, is still recognized as the forerunner of every contemporary work on the French countryside.[133] Combining texts with minute geographical observation, language and scientific techniques, law and literature, *Les caractères* is in many ways the fruition of *L'île de France.* It presents a diachronic interpretation of history that surpasses the mundane and the immediate. It anticipated Fernand Braudel's terms *longue durée* and *très longue durée.*[134] "Human time... will never conform to the inexorable uniformity... of a clock's time. It must have

[131] *Apologie,* pp. 157–58.

[132] Ibid., p. 129.

[133] Bryce Lyon, Foreword to *French Rural History* (U.S. ed.), p. xv, especially n. 10.

[134] *Les caractères originaux,* pp. 250–51, and also "Le salaire et les fluctuations économiques à longue période," *Revue historique* 173 (1934): 1–31. Cf. Fernand Braudel, "Histoire et sciences sociales: La longue durée," *Écrits sur l'histoire* (Paris, 1969).

measurements that are appropriate to its own changeable rhythm ... and limits that, like reality itself, include marginal zones. Only with this plasticity as its model can history hope to adapt its classifications to what Bergson has termed 'an exact measure of reality': which is, after all, the ultimate aim of all knowledge."[135]

Bloch was aware of the revolutionary nature of *Les caractères*. The work would have to be revised and amplified by future scholars. He nonetheless realized that he had attained an extraordinary level of abstraction that allowed him to present a faithful and hitherto unachieved representation of human reality.

The quest for sythesis. Bloch's *Société féodale* is probably his best known historical study. Here he combined the fruits of over thirty years of research, teaching, writing, and contemplation. It was published in the collaborative multivolume series that Henri Berr had launched in 1913 (and which began appearing in 1920). *L'évolution de l'humanité*, whose aim was to go beyond purely monographic history to recapture the complexity of the past. In its two volumes, published in 1939–40, *La société féodale* presents what Bloch considered the essence of medieval Europe: its material conditions, its legal and political bases, and its modes of thought and sentiment.[136]

The work presents many new ideas on social structure, on the supernatural qualities ascribed to Europe's kings, and on the growth of a "national consciousness." Bloch also emphasized that the core of the West's idea of per-

[135] *Apologie*, p. 153.

[136] *La société féodale: La formation des liens de dépendance* (Paris, 1939; 2d ed., Paris, 1949) and *La société féodale: Les classes et le gouvernement des hommes* (Paris, 1940). Published in English as *Feudal Society*, 2 vols., trans. L. A. Manyon (Chicago, 1961).

sonal liberty derived from the unique lord–vassal relationship, an arrangement that was both binding and reciprocal. To Bloch, the "right of resistance" granted to the medieval warrior when his overlord acted contrary to the law was an article of faith and action in his own life. Bloch's formative experiences—as the scholar who sought out the meaning as well as the rituals attached to freedom in medieval Europe, as the *homme disponible* who had served the French Republic in two world wars—are reflected in *La société féodale;* its dominant theme is an ancient maxim of vigilance in the preservation of honor, justice, and liberty. Together with the books Bloch wrote during World War II, *L'étrange défaite* and *Apologie pour l'histoire* (both of which contain explicit reflections on World War I), *La sociéte féodale* represents an eloquent testimony on the impact of the Great War.

Recalling the courage and self-confidence of the *Souvenirs de guerre* ("If I'm not dead in two minutes, I'll be all right"), one may conclude that Marc Bloch emerged from World War I more firm than ever in his conviction of the importance of the individual and the necessity of human freedom. Kierkegaard's *Existenz-philosophie* had entered the mainstream of European philosophy just before World War I, and it flourished immediately afterward. Bloch's life and work epitomize the idealistic stream of existentialism, an acceptance of the reality of one's own mortality while striving through the highest standards of courage and intelligence to transcend the limitations of human existence. To quote a contemporary philosopher: "Fear is an emotion indispensable for survival . . . without [which] no living thing could last long. The courageous man is not one whose soul lacks this emotion or who can overcome it once and for all, but one who has decided that fear is not what he wants to show."[137]

[137] Hannah Arendt, *The Life of the Mind,* vol. 1: *Thinking* (New York, 1978), pp. 36–37.

Memoirs of War, 1914–15

PART I

I had the honor of taking part in the first five months of the campaign of 1914–15. Now on sick leave in Paris, I am gradually recovering from a severe case of typhoid fever, which on January 5, 1915, forced me to leave the front. I intend to use this respite to fix my recollections before their still fresh and vibrant colors fade. I shall not record everything; oblivion must have its share. Yet I do not want to abandon the five astonishing months through which I have just lived to the vagaries of my memory, which has tended in the past to make an injudicious selection, burdening itself with dull details while allowing entire scenes, any part of which would be precious, to disappear. The choice it has exercised so poorly I intend this time to control myself.

I

August 1914! I still see myself standing in the corridor of the train that was bringing my brother and me back from Vevey, where we had learned on July 31 of Germany's declaration of a state of war.* I watched the sun rise in a beautiful, cloudy sky, and I repeated under my breath these rather trivial words, which nevertheless seemed laden with a terrible and hidden meaning: "Behold the dawn of the month of August 1914!" On arriving at the Gare de Lyon in Paris, we learned from the newspapers that Jean Jaurès had been assassinated. To our grief was added a painful doubt. War seemed inevitable. Would riots sully its first moments? Today, everyone knows how groundless these concerns were. Jaurès was gone. The influence of his noble spirit did survive, however, as the reaction of the socialist party demonstrated to the nations of the world.

One of the most beautiful memories the war has given me was the sight of Paris during the first days of mobilization. The city was quiet and somewhat solemn. The drop in traffic, the absence of buses, and the shortage of taxis made the streets almost silent. The sadness that was buried in our hearts showed only in the red and swollen eyes of many women. Out of the specter of war, the nation's armies created a surge of democratic fervor. In Paris there remained only "those who were leaving"—the nobility—and those who were not leaving, who seemed at that moment to recognize no obligation other than to pamper the soldiers of tomorrow. On the streets, in the stores and streetcars, strangers chatted freely; the unanimous goodwill, though often expressed in naive or awkward words and gestures, was nonetheless moving. The men for the most part were not hearty; they were resolute, and that was better.

*Proclaimed that afternoon by Wilhelm II. On August 1 Germany ordered mobilization and declared war on France's ally, Russia.

Very early on the morning of August 4, I left for Amiens.* I went part of the long way between the avenue d'Orléans and the Gare de la Chapelle in a market gardener's wagon that a police constable had requisitioned for my use. Because I sat in the back, wedged between baskets of vegetables, the fresh and slightly acrid odor of cabbage and carrots will always bring back the emotions of that early-morning departure: my enthusiasm and the constriction that gripped my heart. At the Gare de la Chapelle, an aged, white-haired father made heroic but unavailing efforts to hold back his tears as he embraced an artillery officer. At Amiens I found an extraordinarily animated city, its streets predictably teeming with soldiers; yet I have never understood why there were so many pharmacist officers among them.

On August 10, at 1:30 A.M., the 272d regiment, to which I had been assigned as sergeant (18th company, 4th platoon), left Amiens. Marching through suburban streets in the nocturnal silence, we reached the Longueau station, where we entrained for a long, exhausting journey in oppressive dog-day heat. At Sedan we received an official communiqué announcing the capture of Mulhouse. Happy to speak of a victory at the site of a great defeat, I read it to my men while we were still on the train. At Stenay we disembarked.

From August 11 to 21 the regiment remained in the region of the Meuse, first in the valley itself, where we guarded the bridges, and then on the right bank, close to the border. To be sure, I have not retained a very precise memory of this period. Beautiful days, very calm but a bit

*On August 3 Germany had declared war against France and invaded Belgium.

monotonous, were filled with the petty details of camp duties. The sun, the rustic pleasures—fishing, swimming in the river, and dozing on the grass—in addition to the prospect of an unknown countryside that, although lacking color and sparkle, was not devoid of charm, all would have been agreeable enough had they not been permeated by our feverish anticipation.

During the night of the 20th to the 21st, the platoon to which I belonged was quartered in the town hall in Quincy, a village in the northern part of the Woëvre forest. In the middle of the night an officer from staff headquarters appeared in the schoolroom in which we slept. Rudely awakened, our platoon leader jumped into his slippers and went to take the orders of the intruder, who wanted to be conducted to the colonel. The regiment left an hour later. We marched toward the front. In the open country, at the foot of the citadel of Montmédy, whose ancient bastions rose above a grassy escarpment, we first heard the cannon that the troops called "the brute"; and it was on the next day, during a halt, that we saw our first shrapnel as distant white wreaths in an azure sky. On the night of the 21st, we took up quarters in a tiny village next to Montmédy, called Iré-les-Prés; in the morning we left as escort to the supply train of our army corps. We had been told we were about to enter Belgium. I shall never forget the men's joy at this news. On the way a counterorder arrived, and a very long and very hard march brought my company to Velosnes, a village right next to the Belgian border. It was occupied by troops of the fourth regiment, some of whom had just returned from combat. In a house on the small square where the washhouse was located we could see three German prisoners through the window.

We slept huddled together in a cold barn. As for me, stretched out on a pile of twigs, it was not too bad a night.

On the 23rd we encountered the first wounded I had seen during the campaign. Our company was assigned to dig trenches in front of Thonne-la-Long, a village as near to the border as Velosnes, though farther west. It was there, in those trenches we occupied until the morning of the 25th, that I spent my first two nights in the open. I find these words in my journal for August 23: "First day the impression is truly serious.... Many wounded on the roads. We could see beside the road (which was perpendicular to the trenches we were guarding) the remnants of two battalions of the 87th regiment. In sum, the rear of a great battle and, I believe, a great victory. Since the 21st, however, I have known that the Germans are in Brussels."

On the morning of the 25th we beat a retreat, and I realized that the hope expressed in the lines I have just quoted was misplaced. This immensely bitter disappointment, the stifling heat, the difficulties of marching along a road encumbered by artillery and convoys, and finally, the dysentery with which I was stricken the night before make the 25th of August live in my memory as one of the most painful days I have known. Shall I ever forget the two cups of hot coffee that a peasant woman gave me in a village near Han-les-Juvigny, where we happened to stop that day? For obvious reasons, I had had nothing to drink since morning. As long as I live, no liquid will ever give me greater pleasure than those two cups of foul "juice."

We spent the night in a forest. In summer, when the weather is fine, there is no nicer site for a bivouac, or, I believe, any more agreeable place to sleep. The leafy branches of the shelter filter any raw edge from the night

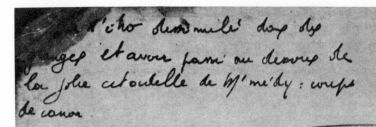

... l'cho dissimulé dans les
granges et avoir passé en dessous de
la jolie citadelle de M'me'dy : coups
de canon.

22. on part le matin à escorte du
train de combat — on va cantonner à
Sommethore en Belgique — joie des
hommes — marche assez dure — canonnade.
on s'arrête en route — vu les premières
fumées de schrapnells — on reprend la
marche — on va à Valonnes. (?) tout près
de la frontière belge — tout le
canon — marche longue et dure — part
le matin à 6 h. on arrive à 7 h — on couche
empilé dans une grange froide — la nuit à
minuit 1/2 départ brusque

23 : première journée où l'impatience est
vraiment pénible — on part le matin rejoindre
le reste du bataillon à Bud. Verneville.

Bloch's journal: August 23, 1914

« puis on va à Rhona les Ard. « on
rencontre bcp de blessés « on fait des
tranchées « comme ~~~~ ~~~~ bcp.
d'isolés sur les routes « on voit les sur
la route les débris de 2 bataillons du 8J :
rst 1 capitaine (que nous ne voyons pas)
1 mgt major, 1 fourrier, 2 sergents ! —
c'est toute l'envers d' 1 qule bataille, —
je crois d'1 qule section — mais depuis
le 21 je vois les Allemands à Bruxelles
99 prisonn.

Orist mon collègue, à la 2e demi section
un bon garçon facile, employé chez un
libraire-juif, vaguement tenté de
littérature.

Marçot : caporal de la 16e neurasthénique
h. du monde, peu guerrier.

_____

VII : 23 au soir au 25 au matin.
toug. ds. les tranchées ; 2 nuits de bivouac
~~~~ nous sommes au contact, nous dit-on
le 24 au soir avec juste 1 cie du 72e en
avant de nous ; la sec. met de
très nombreux malades, je vois qu'une arme

air, and their barely perceptible fragrance lightly perfumes the fresh breezes that occasionally caress the sleeper's face. These slumbers "under the stars," this unencumbered sleep in which the lungs breathe easily, and from which one never awakes with a heavy head, though not deep, still provides pleasures unknown to those who sleep indoors. While we were relishing these charms, the enemy approached.

Owing to a delay in our order to move out, we were almost caught. Our rude awakening was followed by a forced march. On the way, we saw people abandoning their village in haste. Men, women, children, furniture, bundles of linen (and often the most disparate objects!) were piled on their wagons. These French peasants fleeing before an enemy against whom we could not protect them left a bitter impression, possibly the most maddening that the war has inflicted on us. We were to see them often during the retreat, poor refugees crowding the roads and village squares with their wagons. Wrenched from their homes, disoriented, dazed, and bullied by the gendarmes, they were troublesome but pathetic figures. At Baricourt, on the night of the 26th, while we slept in a sort of stable, they slept outside with their carts in the rain, the women holding their babies in their arms. The next morning, while held in reserve on a plateau that dominated the left bank of the Meuse, we watched the smoke from burning villages rise into a shrapnel-speckled sky.

The retreat lasted until September 5, interrupted by a three-day rest in the Grandpré hollow, first at Ternes, then at Grandpré itself, followed by four days of very hard marching. It left me with a vague but generally painful feeling similar to the ache that follows a bad night. The dusty roads along which the company was all too often strung out, the suffocating heat, especially while crossing woods whose meager growth provided little shade yet impeded the rare breaths of fresh air, the extremely late stops for the night and too-early departures, the uncomfortable accommodations, and the monotony of each day, all these would have been minor had we not had our backs constantly turned to the border, continually retreating without fighting. What was happening? We knew absolutely nothing. I suffered acutely from this ignorance. I stand bad news better than uncertainty, and nothing irritates me more than the suspicion that I am being deceived. Oh, what bitter days of retreat, of weariness, boredom, and anxiety!

On September 6 we saw the first wounded of the great battle that was then under way and which would become known to history as the Battle of the Marne. We were in front of the Château du Plessis, near Orconte in Champagne. Some wounded from colonial units passed us on the road, and we gave them something to drink. We were then deployed in a firing line behind a ditch. We thought we were about to go into action. Tired of doing nothing, the men were pleased but also solemn. This, however, proved a false alarm. On the morning of the 7th we moved to Larzicourt, a village of white rock on the right bank of the Marne; there the orchards were laden with delicious plums. We rested for three days, staying in the village only at night. By day we occupied the trenches we had dug in the wheat fields to the north. The weather was warm and beautiful. In front of us a forest hid the horizon. To the left, on the side of Vitry-le-François, in a sky that seemed immense above this flat countryside, we could see shells bursting incessantly in the distance.

On the evening of the 9th, just as my platoon had bed-

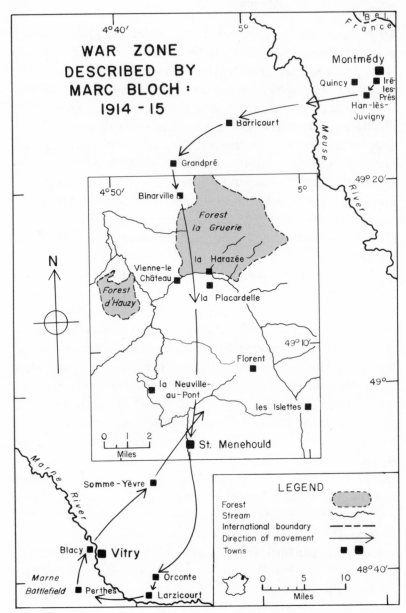

WAR ZONE
DESCRIBED BY
MARC BLOCH:
1914 - 15

War zone described by Bloch

ded down in our hayloft, we were awakened by an alert.
Our regiment joined a long infantry column, and an interminable nocturnal march began. On leaving Larzicourt,
we crossed the Marne. I believed our trenches were intended to cover, if necessary, a retreat beyond the river,
and were therefore to be held at all costs and abandoned
only after a total defeat. Hadn't we read at Larzicourt
Joffre's order "to die on the spot rather than yield"? But
now it seemed the great retreat had begun, since we were
crossing the bridge we had been ordered to defend. Once
more we resumed the long, dreary movement to the rear
which had taken us from the border of Belgian Luxem-
bourg to the Marne. So many times we had hoped to see it
end: at the Meuse, at Grandpré, at almost all the villages
in which we had billeted for a night, and finally, in the
trenches of Larzicourt. Now once again we moved on. I
believed all was lost. Had I only known! That night I sadly
made my way along a tortuously winding road beside
which clusters of trees took on a ghostly air against the
dark sky; with anger in my heart, feeling the weight of the
rifle I had never fired, and hearing the faltering footsteps
of our half-sleeping men echo on the ground, I could only
consider myself one more among the inglorious van-
quished who had never shed their blood in combat. Yet
back in Paris, at General Staff headquarters, they recognized, or at least suspected, victory. At Larzicourt, however, we knew nothing. On that march I suffered through
long, painful hours.

Eventually, however, despite our endless detours, I
realized that we were no longer heading southwest. I
began to suspect that we were participating not in a retreat
but in one of those troop movements that occur so frequently on arrival at a field of battle. This was true. As

dawn approached, a heavy, chilling rain began to fall. We continued to march, despite our extreme fatigue and empty stomachs. One man found a German helmet, and we all tried it on in turn to relieve our boredom. At a crossroads we were met by an automobile. An officer from headquarters got out, spoke with our colonel for a few minutes, and then dashed off. We left the road through some high, soaked grasses on the right and climbed a steep slope. Abandoning our normal formation (in column), we shifted to one of platoons, four lines abreast, which regulations prescribe for troops approaching the line of fire under the threat of enemy artillery. Before reaching the crest, the regiment halted, and we were ordered to kneel. Day was breaking. The air was fresh. The rain had just stopped. Our damp capes were heavy. I was no longer sleepy. Our lieutenant left to see the captain or the battalion commander, I no longer remember which, and when he returned said, "You are about to fight. You have wanted this for a long time."

Resuming our march, we crossed the ridge and dropped into a valley that followed a road. We stopped again along its edge. On the left we could see the buildings of a farm, called, I believe, the Grand Perthes. The halt lasted a good while, perhaps an hour. The men were calm and a little pale. Our old captain, more shaken than ever, lit a pipe with the remark that it might well be his last. A lieutenant protested politely. I opened a can of cherry jam that the company's cyclist had picked up in some village the night before and passed it around. The first large shells arrived with a whistle. They fell a few hundred meters away, giving off heavy black smoke. A cow was killed and a man nearby. Then we began to move forward again, leaving the road and climbing the slope opposite the one by which we had come. We then passed a line of trenches occupied by another regiment, the 100th, I believe.

It is likely that as long as I live, at least if I do not become senile in my last days, I shall never forget the 10th of September, 1914. Even so, my recollections of that day are not altogether precise. Above all they are poorly articulated, a discontinuous series of images, vivid in themselves but badly arranged like a reel of movie film that showed here and there large gaps and the unintended reversal of certain scenes. On that day, under extremely violent fire from heavy artillery and machine guns, we advanced a few kilometers—at least three or four—from ten in the morning until six at night. Our losses were severe; my company alone, which was certainly not the worst hit, suffered almost one-third casualties. If my memory is correct, the time did not seem long; indeed, those dreadful hours must have passed fairly quickly. We advanced on an undulating field, at first dotted with clumps of trees, then completely bare. I recall that while crossing a hedge, I sharply questioned a man who had stopped. He answered, "I've been wounded." In fact, though he had not actually been hit, he had been stunned by the blast of a shell. He was the first to be hurt. Farther on I noticed the first body, a corporal who did not belong to our regiment. He lay on a slope all rigid with his face down, while around him were scattered some potatoes that had escaped from his camp kettle, which had opened as he fell. Machine gun bullets rustled through the branches like swarms of wasps. The heavy detonations of the shells shook the air, followed by the chorus of bursts that accompanied each explosion. The shrapnel shell, in particular, vibrates gently while tumbling through the air, only to stop abruptly at the end of its fall. How many of those murderous melodies did I hear on that day! I hunched my head between my shoulders, awaiting the silence and perhaps the fatal blow.

Behind one of the small woods I lost my platoon, but I found it again farther on. The men were lying face down on the yellow earth. Behind us the colonel had been knocked over by a large shell, but he got up and rejoined us unhurt. Next to me a corporal had been wounded in the arm and knee. The other platoon leader and I began bandaging his wounds, but were both hit: my colleague fairly seriously in the thigh, I only slightly in the right arm. The bullet, after piercing my sleeve, had the decency to exit immediately, merely burning my skin. Since the pain was severe, I first thought I was seriously injured, but then quickly realized that it was nothing. At about the same time, a sudden panic gripped our platoon, caused, as far as I can remember, by some machine gunners' horses. Someone had stupidly brought the guns up there to establish a battery, which was quite impossible under such a hail of fire. The animals stampeded and spread confusion among the rest of us. I still see myself running, upright, trying to get away from two horses that for some inexplicable reason seem prodigiously large in my memory. I also recall shouting, "Don't panic. Above all, don't panic, or we're lost." Then, on our lieutenant's order, we all rushed toward the right to reach a ridge behind which the next platoons had already taken cover. Quartermaster S. was settled there, half seated, half reclining against the slope. As I passed at top speed, he shouted at me to dive into the ditch in front of him, and I followed his excellent advice.

How long did we stay in that fold in the earth? How many minutes, or how many hours, I am not sure. We were crowded against each other and piled one on top of another. Since the enemy artillery had us under fire on the right flank, the slope in front offered us illusory protection at best. Many men were killed or wounded. For some time I had on my right our chief sergeant major, a big blond fellow with an open manner and a peasant's speech. He had been hit on the hand; a blood-soaked rag reddened his fingers. The wound was light. The poor man was killed toward the end of the day, but by then I had lost track of him. I was half lying on my neighbor to the left. I think I have never detested anyone so much as that individual, whom I had never seen before that day, never met again, and doubtless would not recognize if I ever should meet him in the future. He had cramps in his legs, on which I was lying, and he insisted that to relieve him I should raise myself, although this would have needlessly exposed me to death. I am still glad I refused, and I hope the self-centered clod suffers often from rheumatism. In front of me, next to S., my company's adjutant was seated with his back against the slope; although he had placed his haversack on his head for added protection, he trembled each time a shell whistled by. The wounded cried out. One of them begged the colonel alternately first to help him, then to finish him off. I believe I was quite calm. The spirit of curiosity, which rarely deserts me, had not disappeared. I remember first noting that the smoke from time shells was an ochre color, as distinguished from the black fumes of the percussion shells. I nevertheless found war an ugly business, the faces of men awaiting and dreading death not beautiful to behold, and I vaguely recalled some pages from Tolstoy.

The colonel was on my left together with his adjutant. With one knee on the ground, he was attempting to see over the ridge. He was pale and seemed undecided. Finally he ordered an advance. A few of our regiment had pushed on ahead of us and we had to catch up with them. I said "ordered," but "beseeched" would be more accurate. "Let's go, boys, we must move forward. Your comrades are out there in front. They're firing. You can't leave them alone. Noncoms, lead the way!" It was hard to leave our slope. I have already explained why it gave only meager protection, but we nonetheless had felt ourselves more secure than we really were. We had confidence in this chance cover, poor as it was, and we were filled with a quite understandable reluctance to launch ourselves upright into open space. I remember thinking very clearly at that moment, "Since the colonel wants it, we must get up and go forward. But it's all over, there's no use hoping. I will be killed." Then we rose and ran. I shouted, "Forward, Eighteenth!" We reached a path that followed a slight rise in the ground. There, finding a small group of soldiers, we stopped. Beyond the irregularly tufted grass that covered the crest of the slope, we could see a wide landscape. With good eyesight, apparently, it was possible to make out the enemy's positions. The officers ordered us to open fire. My arm being too painful to manage my rifle, I simply transmitted the orders. In any case, firing over such a long distance at objects so difficult to see was undoubtedly ineffective. Some men near me were wounded. The day was nearly over. We prayed for the arrival of complete darkness, which would end the fighting. The German bombardment gradually slowed. At the same time, our guns picked up the pace. What joy to hear not German but French shells whistling above us and aimed at the enemy! As evening fell, I risked leaving the shelter of the slope to go to one of our corporals who lay seriously wounded a

few meters behind. I could not do much for him. At nightfall I ordered two of his men to carry him to an ambulance;
but unable to get through, they finally had to abandon him
along the way. In the deepening dusk the regiment fell
back to the embankment where our last advance had begun.

It was there that we spent the night. From time to time a
few bullets whistled by. About 10 P.M., I believe, the German machine guns resumed firing, without doing us any
harm. They soon fell silent. We were famished. I had a can
of sardines; I opened it, ate a few, and shared the rest. It
was cold. During the summer campaign we had never
before experienced such chill. The wounded screamed or
groaned. Many asked for something to drink. We organized a fatigue party to get water, but despite a long
search it found nothing. Its return caused an alarm and, I
suspect, drew some rifle fire. Later during the night we
had several anxious moments. I recall getting myself up to
order the men, who had been more or less assembled, to
fix their bayonets, though after a sleepless night followed
by a rough day they would probably have offered feeble
resistance to any attack. The smell of blood permeated the
air. Yet despite this stale odor, despite the cries and the
groans, despite our fears, I slept for a few hours, stretched
out in a furrow.

Shortly before daybreak, the order came for us to return
to the rear. We reached the valley where we had spent the
evening before going into combat. The colonel commanding our brigade passed on horseback. He congratulated
us, shouting, "Vive le 272!" and informed us that the
Germans had retreated. Since we had nothing to eat, he
ordered the lieutenant who was acting as commander of
the company in place of our wounded captain to kill one

cow and one sheep from the flocks that were wandering scattered and bewildered, with no shepherds, on the hill behind us. These innocent victims were put to death with revolver shots. During the morning I went to visit the field hospital, where one of the wounded had asked for me. There I saw injuries and faces in agony. The men did not cry out, as they had done the day before on the battlefield. They barely moaned, and their faces spoke more of weariness than of suffering.

Despite so many painful sights, it does not seem to me that I was sad on that morning of September 11. Needless to say, I did not feel like laughing. I was serious, but my solemnity was without melancholy, as befitted a satisfied soul; and I believe that my comrades felt the same. I recall their faces, grave yet content. Content with what? Well, first content to be alive. It was not without a secret pleasure that I contemplated the large gash in my canteen, the three holes in my coat made by bullets that had not injured me, and my painful arm, which, on inspection, was still intact. On days after great carnage, except for particularly painful personal grief, life appears sweet. Let those who will condemn this self-centered pleasure. Such feelings are all the more solidly rooted in individuals who are ordinarily only half aware of their existence. But our good humor had another, more noble source. The victory that the colonel had announced to us so briefly as he trotted by had elated me. Perhaps if I had thought about it, I might have felt some doubts. The Germans had retreated before us, but how did I know they had not advanced elsewhere? Happily, my thoughts were vague. The lack of sleep, the exertions of the march and combat, and the strain of my emotions had tired my brain; but my sensations were vivid. I had little comprehension of the battle. It was the

Ruins of the village of Perthes (Battle of the Marne)

victory of the Marne, but I would not have known what to call it. What matter, it was victory. The bad luck that had weighed us down since the beginning of the campaign had been lifted. My heart beat with joy that morning in our small, dry, devastated valley in Champagne.

II

The morning of September 11 was spent taking stock of our losses. The regiment was without its colonel, the fifth battalion—my own—had lost its major, and in the 18th company we had no captain. Fortunately, these three officers were only wounded. The commander of the sixth battalion assumed control of the regiment. Of the four captains of the fifth battalion, two had been wounded, one was dead, and the one who survived untouched took over the functions of battalion commander, with the result that the four companies were placed under the orders of lieutenants, most of whom (and ours was the first) thereby earned their third stripes.

At 11 A.M. we set off again. We took the same direction as the day before but bore to the right. We crossed a corner of the battlefield where teams of soldiers were gathering up the last wounded, both French and German, and burying the dead. Many bodies still lay on the ground where they had fallen in complete exhaustion, their muscles contracted as if making a final effort. Those who die in great battles do not know the majesty of eternal rest. The stench turns one's stomach. The ground was strewn with all sorts of debris, weapons, equipment, and human fragments. I saw a severed leg that lay far from its body, alone and almost ridiculous amid the horror. Passing quickly, we finally left that funereal scene behind us.

The march, although not particularly long, seemed

hard. We followed the gloomy valleys of Champagne on weary legs, but with good heart. We were in pursuit. Baskets full of abandoned shells at German gun replacements; empty trenches around which we marched; wheels of wagons and bicycles thrown on the edge of the road and into the deep ruts that slowed our steps, all told us of the retreat—if not rout—of the enemy. During a halt at the entrance to the village of Blacy, a few shells fell on a neighboring ridge, reminding us again of his artillery. We spent the night at a nearby farm. The entire battalion was billeted in a barn, with the result that we had to crowd in this way and that to take the least space possible. The Germans had occupied the same quarters the night before. Underneath the straw, which reeked of absinthe, we found half-empty bottles.

Not for long did our weary limbs rest in that foul-smelling litter. On September 12, at a quarter past four in the morning, when it was still dark, we set out on a terrible day's march. We were, in fact, in full pursuit of the Germans. Along the side of the road their fires were still warm. During our short halts we ransacked their campsites, and to our amusement turned up a mass of odds and ends. In one place I recall finding a violin. We laughed easily. That morning, under beautiful, clear skies, we crossed the valley of the Marne. Its white villages and shaded roads were pleasant to see after the mournful solitude of the high plains of Champagne. Beside the pleasant road, in the ditch, under the cottonwoods that grew along the embankment, lay a chasseur and his horse, both covered with blood. On the right bank we returned to the plateau, its broad undulations blanketed with an unusual grass and dotted by sparse woods that broke the monotony of its vast horizon. Along that chalky road the brigade stretched out in an interminable column. A storm was gathering in the dark sky. We were hot and thirsty. During the long halt I threw myself on the ground, exhausted. Even so, I have a pleasant memory of that rough day. We were in pursuit.

At a crossroads we met a small group of peasants, hostages the Germans had just released. My God, how happy those poor people were! Farther on, toward evening, we left the main road and proceeded across the fields to our left in combat formation. We continued in that manner toward the town of Somme-Yèvre, which our officers believed was still occupied by a German cavalry division. It began to rain, and a thick mud clung to our boots. The men grumbled. A fight would undoubtedly have dispelled their bad humor, but that was not to be. On the outskirts of the village we learned the Germans had left, apparently about 2 P.M. Somme-Yèvre was virtually deserted. We had to improvise a billet in the dark. We were assigned to abandoned houses that the Germans had occupied before us. As usual we recognized their remains. My platoon did not, like many of our comrades, have to clean up the excrement of our enemies. Nevertheless, before settling ourselves we had to stuff back into the closets all the linens they had pulled out and strewn around the house. We needed food, so some sheep were killed. Each platoon received one. For some inexplicable reason, we of the fourth platoon ended up with two. By the paltry light of a few lamps, our cooks carved them up on a dining room table, producing a bloody spectacle of preparations for a barbarous feast, which seemed nevertheless agreeable enough to my famished stomach.

We stayed in Somme-Yèvre most of the next day. I read a pulp novel called *The Mysteries of the Inquisition* which I had found in some corner. Troops of all services passed through the town in incessant waves. A cavalry colonel asked one of our men for a piece of bread. About four o'clock our regiment moved out. There were German corpses along the side of the road. The march lasted into the night. I was weary and footsore. The men were exhausted. I was plodding on, back bent, generally uncomfortable, and hoping only for the next hourly halt, when an escaped horse created an absurd alert in our column. Everyone thought it was the Uhlans. Our men threw themselves off the road. The second lieutenant in command of our platoon was pushed into the ditch. I myself was half dragged, half carried into a field by a force that was all the more irresistible because it was so sudden. I had to rally my men as best I could and make them fix their bayonets, less to ward off a danger in which I scarcely believed than to restore their confidence and prevent them from shooting at random and injuring one another. A shot had already been fired, but order was finally restored. The incident was unfortunate, and we had no desire to recall it later. In the middle of the night we reached the village of Elise, where we slept.

Of the three following days—September 14, 15, and 16—I have retained a confused and none too agreeable impression. We were in the vicinity of Ste-Menehould, and we did not move far. For the most part, we were stationed in the fields, guarding batteries of artillery or simply awaiting orders. We returned late to our quarters. Ordinarily there was only the small end of a candle to illuminate an entire barn, and we had to settle ourselves mostly by groping. The weather was bad, with frequent rain. During our long halts we clumsily built shelters of branches, which, because of our lack of experience, gave

French defensive emplacements in the forest of Hauzy, 1914

but poor protection. The dampness penetrated our clothing. The roads, which had been battered four times, first
by our armies in retreat, then by the conquering Germans,
afterward by the German retreat, and finally by our van-
guard in pursuit of the enemy, were nothing but extended
bogs. I was tired and had a touch of fever. The enthusiasm
of victory was gone. We were no longer advancing. We
heard cannonades, often very heavy. We spent long hours
listening to them without moving, without knowing anything of what was taking place around us, and expecting
we knew not what.

We spent the morning of September 16 in the rain
guarding a battery in a hollow. Around three in the afternoon, the regiment received an order to go and help the
troops defending the forest of Hauzy. This wood, with
few large trees and sparse underbrush, covered the highest point of the terrain that separates the Aisne and the
Tourbe, just south of their confluence. The railway between Ste-Menehould and Vouziers crossed it, and it was
by following the tracks that we proceeded. Because of
some carelessness, the details of which escape me but the
result of which I remember well, we were spotted by the
German guns. I can still see us running along the roadbed,
stumbling over the ties to the noise of the shells. The
Germans aimed badly. None of us was hit.

My memories of this first sojourn in the forest of Hauzy
are primarily meteorological. Our company was placed in
reserve in the middle of the forest near a grade crossing.
Shells were falling heavily, the enemy trying to concentrate his fire on the rail line. On the 17th we were no little
surprised to see an unfamiliar civilian appear in our lines;
he seemed to have lost the power of speech, but his ges-

tures expressed great excitement. He was the wagon driver who brought our provisions. A percussion bomb had fallen almost on top of him, killing six soldiers who were having a snack. Panic-stricken, the poor man had fled, abandoning his horse and wagon. Fortunately, the quartermaster sergeant who had accompanied him retained more self-possession and stayed to guard our bread. Otherwise our comrades in the colonial regiments, who were garrisoned in the woods along with us, would no doubt have cleaned us out.

None of us had yet been seriously wounded. Though we were well aware of the shells, we really thought only of the rain. Inexhaustible clouds dumped an almost incessant downpour on the underbrush. The clay soil held the water on its surface. Our trenches were a brook, the woodland roads were lakes of mud, and the ditches alongside were tumbling torrents of a yellowish flood. Whenever the rain stopped for a few minutes, we immediately lit fires, roasting our coats and our boots to try to dry them. The nights were chilly. We bade goodbye to the beautiful August nights, so pleasant for sleeping under the stars. Autumn was coming and bringing with it the bitter edge of the first frost. We had clumsily constructed shelters out of branches, but their skimpy and uneven surfaces let the rain through; I can remember the misery of waking up completely chilled. I also remember one particular night, that of the 17th to the 18th, which by extraordinary chance was completely dry. I was guarding the tracks with the first squad, of which I was in command. The sky was unusually clear, the wind from the north. Not wishing to wear my coat, which had been soaked by the day's rains, I stretched it out on the ground. Wearing only my jacket, I did not dare lie down for fear of catching cold. I spent the entire night on my feet, feeling as though I were naked in an icy bath.

During the next months we would experience even more severe temperatures and more penetrating dampness, and today I find it difficult to understand why we should have suffered so much in that wretched wood of Hauzy. Yet there is an explanation. We were very inexperienced. We were poorly nourished, and at that time our provisioning functioned most unsatisfactorily. But above all, still clothed in the uniforms in which we had started out, without sweaters, blankets, or raincoats, we were as poorly equipped as southerners thrown abruptly into the hoarfrosts of the north.

Toward evening on September 20 we were relieved by the 328th. We would sleep at La Neuville-au-Pont. I read in my journal for that date: "A barn, what luxury!"

La Neuville-au-Pont was to remain our home base from September 21 through October 1. Consequently, as will be seen, we returned there often. La Neuville was a good-sized market town where the Second Corps maintained its staff headquarters during its stay in the Argonne. It was split in two by the Aisne. The main part of town was situated on the steep slopes of the right bank, while the railroad station, at the end of an avenue shaded by lovely trees, was on the left. From the lane where we regularly stayed, an extremely steep and slippery little path, flanked by scraggly bushes, led to the riverbank. We went that way whenever we had a chance to wash. On a few occasions I followed the river downstream, where it flowed among tree stumps, sometimes very shallow but sometimes almost full enough to flood its banks, according to whether the sluices upstream were closed or opened.

The church stood in the middle of the main square. It

La-Neuville-au-Pont: church

was very old, its basic structure dating from the finest Gothic period. Its plan was simple, without a transept. The central nave was topped by two plain steeples, which rested firmly on the two aisles. The solid buttresses, which the master masons of the area had chosen over the lighter but more difficult flying buttress, provided the external support for the weight of the roof. Sober, robust, perhaps somewhat squat, it was definitely a country church. Yet it had some elegant features: its handsome Gothic western door and the north and south doors, where the Renaissance appeared. All three, very ornate but not excessively so, were charming in their delicacy and vigor. I never remember the church at Neuville without emotion. More than once, on returning from the trenches, I went there to attend services being held for the men of the 272d who had just fallen. I still see its modest nave, its whitewashed arches, its heavy wooden benches where the soldiers sat in crowded rows, and also the solemn faces of those near me, tired and somewhat sleepy, because it was morning and, having spent the preceding night on the front line, we were all badly in need of rest. I have always believed it a pious duty to remember our dead. But what did the rituals mean to me?

From September 21 to October 1, we moved about a great deal without accomplishing much of anything. We usually slept at La Neuville-au-Pont. There was one exception, when we spent two nights, the 24th and 25th, closer to the enemy at the farm called Moulinet. We were being used to dig reserve trenches in the rear, to occupy backup positions behind the line of fire, and to guard the generals' observation posts. Occasionally we performed fatigue duty in Neuville itself. We never knew the day before what we would be doing on the morrow. Our or-

La-Neuville-au-Pont: street scene

La-Neuville-au-Pont: soldiers in camp

ders usually arrived in the middle of the night. We never knew in the afternoon where we would be lodged that evening. We set out early and returned late, well after dark. We had to wait a long time for our supper before being able to go to bed in the straw. A tiring existence but at the same time almost pointless. We were relieved on two occasions, on the 23rd and the 26th. I read in my journal for the 23rd: "Day of rest in quarters," that is, in La Neuville-au-Pont: sun, cleaning the thick crust of mud with which we were still covered (we had not yet been able to rid ourselves of this filth since our return from the Hauzy forest), letters, a rabbit; such were the rather dreary pleasures of this respite.

In addition to these official rest periods, we were often idle. I had neither books nor newspapers; only much later were newpapers sold in La Neuville. Except for a few letters, I knew practically nothing of what had been taking place on the various battle fronts. This ignorance annoyed and worried me. Yet one should not infer that these days, so repetitious and so empty, left only bad memories. Depending on the state of the weather, changing with the first days of autumn but normally rather mild; on the letters I received with joy or awaited with impatience; on the mysterious reactions of body and soul, which come to the same thing; on the way the passing moments affected us, the hours slipped by agreeably enough or very slowly and painfully. I remember some halts in the fields that seemed pleasant. The grass and the underbrush had begun to turn. The sun was barely warm, the shade already cool. We lit some campfires. The wind blew back the smoke, and its woodsy odor was good to breathe. For all its essential monotony, however, our life was not altogether free of danger. We had two untoward incidents.

On September 24 our company was divided. The first platoon occupied trenches in the rear. The second, in which I served, spent the entire day behind a small wood very close to the Moulinet farm, where we had slept. The weather was beautiful. It was pleasant to stretch out on the grassy slopes. In the evening we returned to the farm, where we joined our comrades and learned that a shell that had fallen on the other platoon as it was preparing to leave the trench had claimed three victims: one wounded, whom we did not believe would survive, and who in fact did die that night, and two killed, including our sergeant major, who had just been promoted two days before. After nightfall we buried them at the edge of a neighboring wood. The gravediggers lighted their work with candles. The second platoon paid their respects. When the bodies were lowered into the grave, the battalion commander said a few words of farewell. He told us that those who had just been buried had found a glorious death and that a similar end awaited us all.

During the afternoon of the 29th, we dug trenches on a ridge in full sunlight. An enemy plane came and hovered overhead. Why was a plane necessary? With a good pair of fieldglasses the Germans could have watched us dig from their own lines. It was a position we should have worked only at night. Shortly after three o'clock a large shell exploded about 150 meters in front of us, emitting a huge cloud of black smoke. A few minutes later a second arrived, with a loud whistle. It fell directly into a trench we had just finished and in which some of our men had sought shelter. At the command of the lieutenant, our platoon fell back behind the ridge in fairly good order while the rest of the company fled to the right, into the woods. Shells continued to fall on the ground we had just abandoned, but at fairly long intervals. We had left a few of our comrades up there, dead or wounded, we did not know. One of the wounded joined us, but we still had some missing.

The lieutenant and I argued over who would climb back up the ridge. He won, since I was obviously obliged to obey him. My obedience, however, was not as complete as it should have been. After sending the platoon toward the foot of the hill, I returned to the scene of the disaster. The lieutenant had found two men stretched out motionless on the ground. Believing both dead, he called to the battalion medical officer, who was arriving with his stretcher bearers, "I have two dead." But one of the bodies rose up and shouted, "I'm not dead!" He was only wounded, though quite badly. The other, unfortunately (a miner from Pas-de-Calais and the father of four children), was indeed dead. The lieutenant and I climbed back down toward our platoon. A few tools and pieces of equipment had been left near our half-dug trenches. We had to send some men to recover them. Shells were falling more heavily. The enemy artillery had lengthened its range and now reached the road that ran along the foot of the hill where we had taken refuge. We were forced to seek shelter in a small wood. We had lost the company and had considerable difficulty reestablishing contact with it. Finally we succeeded, and the captain was able to bring us back under his orders. After a long trek over difficult paths, which the deepening dusk made particularly unpleasant, we rejoined the regiment.

The 272d was still commanded by the same major who had succeeded the colonel on September 11. I would not wish to be too hard on the memory of an officer who later, in November, died honorably of a wound received while charging at the head of his troops in La Gruerie. Yet I would hardly shock anyone who knew him by saying he was a bit unbalanced. On that particular evening he behaved very stupidly. He accused us of having abandoned our post, and he had the bad taste to deliver a public rebuke to our lieutenant right on the road in front of the platoon. The men were incensed. It was a sorry end to a sorry day.

On October 1—the opening day of classes—we returned to the forest of Hauzy, which we entered under a clear moon. Once again we were being held in reserve. Until the evening of the 4th we occupied some narrow but almost watertight burrows near the eastern edge. Those three days passed without incident. Everyone began to realize, however, that we had to expect a winter campaign when the first woolen underwear was distributed.

We spent the 5th and 6th at La Neuville. On the morning of the 7th, my half platoon, which was guarding the road to the cemetery, was replaced by some militiamen. It was the first time we had seen these older comrades so close to the front. A short march brought us to Florent, where we stayed until the 11th. I have a most pleasant memory of this interlude. Florent is a charming spot with huge trees, whose foliage, already tinted yellow and red, shaded the vast square in front of the church. Meadows filled with apple trees surrounded the village. Beyond this belt of orchards lay the woods, which were especially thick to the north. To the south the landscape was cut by a steep valley, in which clear springs gushed in the grass at the foot of the underbrush. It was there that we went each morning to wash.

In Florent we led a nocturnal existence. During the day we slept in our barn, or occupied ourselves with one or

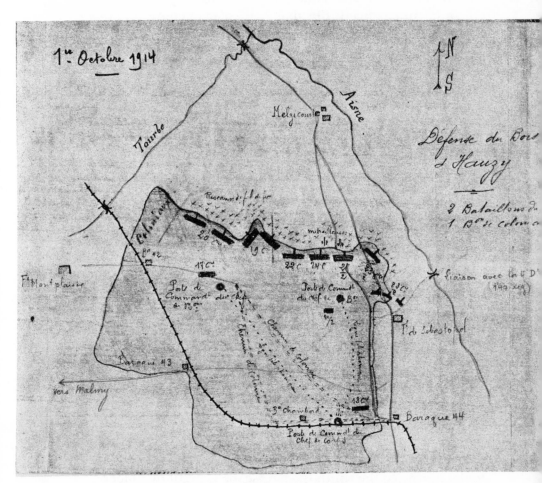

272d Regiment map: defensive emplacements at the forest of Hauzy,
October 1, 1914

Florent: main square and fountain

Florent: mobile kitchen

another of the thousand small tasks about the camp, or roamed idly about the village. In the houses I saw fine rustic furniture made of the wood of the Argonne. At night we would take off toward the north, through the woods, to dig trenches along the edge of a clearing beside the road to La Placardelle. The men worked under the direction of noncommissioned officers of the engineers. As an infantry sergeant, I had virtually nothing to do, but I was not bored. I walked along the road, rested occasionally, chatted with some comrades, daydreamed, and amused myself with the play of the pale nighttime glimmers in the thickets and fields. I enjoyed the calm of the night and its silence, which was now and then broken either by the explosion of shells on our left or by distant rifle fire. Despite these sounds of combat, it was all in all a peaceful, rustic existence, which recalled the one we had known during the first days of the war along the Meuse. It did not last long. On the evening of the 11th, we left for the trenches in the forest of La Gruerie.

III

We left Florent at nightfall and slept at the hamlet of La Placardelle, in a huge barn filled with fodder. I found these quarters less than reassuring. La Placardelle was an ammunition dump. Had even the smallest shell fallen on our hayloft, we would all have been fried before we could have cried out. We left before dawn. In the first light, while descending the steep slope that forms the northern end of the plateau of La Placardelle, I saw for the first time the gracious valley of La Harazée, a view that was to become so familiar to our eyes. It unrolled its long, sinuous ribbon of meadows between hills, almost all of which were covered with trees. On the right, behind the houses of La

La Harazée

La Harazée: mobile kitchen near a shell hole

La Harazée: daybreak at camp

Harazée, where the underbrush covered a steep slope, was La Gruerie. After a halt of some hours, we entered on horribly rough and slippery paths.

We relieved the 128th. My company was stationed on both sides of a wagon track that led toward the enemy. One platoon, designated as the reserve, was stationed on the edge of the same track, just behind the front line. The captain remained with it. The three other platoons moved forward; the fourth (to which I was attached) settled on the right. We reached our places under shellfire. We had counted on finding trenches. We were disappointed to discover only sharpshooters' foxholes, disconnected from one another, too narrow to hold more than two men, and so shallow that to be sheltered one would practically have to lie prone. Our predecessors could hardly have blistered their hands on the handles of their shovels. We established ourselves as well as possible and set to work to improve our situation. The Germans were out there, no doubt quite close. But how far? I had no idea. The underbrush, still thick and only slightly yellowing, hid them.

The afternoon was calm. Stretched out in my hole, I read a novel. A comrade who had stolen it from the school library in La Neuville-au-Pont had lent it to me. I have forgotten the author's name and have lost all recollection of the plot. I'm afraid it was a rather colorless work. Evening fell, bringing with it the anxiety that the deepening shadows cannot fail to arouse in the hearts of inexperienced soldiers, stationed for the first time near the enemy, particularly if they are, as we were, in the middle of a wood. We dreaded a surprise attack. The thickness of the underbrush made the darkness all the blacker. Night is not silent in the forest. The rustling of branches, the light grating of the dry leaves tossed to the ground by the wind, and the occasional sounds of wings and paws, all this music of the shadows, so faint but incessant, disturbed us. We were afraid we would not hear the Germans in time if they advanced. If we had been wise, we would have awaited the dawn in peace. Today I realize that the Germans did not dream of attacking us that night. Indeed, from time to time, without leaving their trenches, they fired a few routine shots intended less to hit us than to keep up their spirits. Our behavior, I regret to report, was quite insane. Taking these harmless gestures seriously, we responded with a furious fusillade. Naturally, they answered in kind, though weakly and without conviction. We began again, more vigorously than ever. No one could aim. If our bullets hit anyone, it could only have been some peaceable service personnel in the rear, a few kilometers behind the German lines, because we were aiming much too high. Moreover, our opponents were neither more skillful nor more careful than we. Almost the entire night was passed in the middle of an infernal racket: detonations, whistling bullets, and commands to "Fire!" The sole result of all this hubbub was to make it impossible to sleep, although it would have been easy, by establishing rotating guard duty, to give each of us a few hours' rest. The moon, appearing toward midnight, enabled us to see across the underbrush, and, by reassuring us with its light, produced some measure of calm. Nevertheless, we stopped wasting our cartridges only at dawn. Such was our first night in the trenches, and I should not hold it up as a model. The captain sent word to us to be less prodigal with our ammunition in the future.

On the next day—it was October 13—the platoon that had until then been waiting in reserve came to relieve us, and we took their place, which we held until the next day.

Entrance to La Gruerie

We stayed in huts made of leafy branches in a clearing near the footpath. Some dirt had been thrown on the roofs and walls and some of the ground underneath had been scooped out, providing at best distinctly poor protection. What always gave the forest of La Gruerie its unique quality, even in its calmest moments, was the stray shots, usually German but occasionally French, which constantly whistled between the trees, menacing the stroller at every step. Their music became so familiar that we quickly stopped paying any attention to them. The most dangerous hours were those following sunset. Then there was always an attack under way in some part of the woods, producing a hail of bullets. On the night of the 13th, the clearing where we were quartered was exceptionally exposed. Spread out flat on my face next to F., the sergeant of the second half platoon, in the hut we shared, I listened to the noisy flight of bullets passing over us as they easily pierced our thin walls.

Toward noon on the 14th we returned to the front line, this time on the left of the company, a position we would not leave until the 20th, the day we quit the woods. We were to be relieved earlier but circumstances, as we shall see, would make all movement of troops impossible for two days. The disposition of the platoon was as follows: On the right, around the path, the second half platoon (the 15th and 16th squads) was protecting a machine gun. A few meters back on the same path, the platoon leader, a second lieutenant, was in a shelter. Then on the left, down an incline that descended toward the ravine of St-Hubert, the first half platoon, which I commanded, was divided between two trenches: one occupied by the 13th squad and the other, the farthest to the left, by the 14th, which I joined. Between the trenches of the second half platoon

Trenchwork in La Gruerie

and that of the 13th squad and between the trench of the 13th squad and mine, there were thirty or forty meters of undefended woods. On my left, almost the same distance away, was the first trench of the neighboring company, the 20th. From one trench to another there were no lines of communication. To transmit orders or reports, to carry ammunition or supplies, we had to move in the open, exposed to the enemy's fire and often to his view.

The Germans were extremely close, scarcely fifty meters away. And the trenches themselves, in what terrible condition we found them! Mine was a sort of narrow furrow, level with the ground, completely straight, and without any screen against shell splinters, so that the fragments of a bomb exploding at one end could easily reach the other, and so shallow that even at best it was necessary to crouch to be safe. Toward the left, our predecessors had dug so little that we at once had to abandon hope of using that section. We intended little by little to push in that direction as we made progress in the digging project we had undertaken. We spent a lot of effort, especially during the first days, to make our hole safer and more comfortable, but as we had nothing but hand tools, we could not accomplish very much. Moreover, the proximity of the enemy and our lack of personnel hardly allowed us to attempt any major enterprise.

One day I received an order to build a shelter in the woods behind us. I went to select the site and took two men with me to begin the work. No sooner had they started than a shrapnel burst in the branches next to us. This might have been an accident, and I refused to let the men halt their work. In a few minutes a second shrapnel showered us with its fragments. We had evidently been spotted. To continue would have caused us to be killed for no purpose. We returned to our places. A few days later I went there again. The Germans, unaware that we had left, had continued to shell the spot. In place of underbrush, there was only a clearing.

To protect the front of our trenches and to set up obstacles in the gaps between them, we were given wire. We did not yet have American barbed wire, only a plain strand without any points, such as was used in the country to hang doorbells or to train vines up walls. I assigned two men to string the wire. The task was not without danger, and they were not happy to have been chosen. Yet afterward they felt decidedly proud of themselves and very ready to recall the episode. In any case, they did their best. I accompanied them with loaded rifle in hand, ready to shoot if by chance we met a German at a turn in the woods. I also remember fastening strands of wire around some empty cans that I placed on the ground in front of us, hoping they might trip any advancing enemies and betray them by the noise. What unnecessary anxiety those wretched cans would cause us later! The wind, or a branch falling from a nearby tree, would cause them to clatter from time to time, and clenching our rifles, we would exclaim: "The enemy!"

The first three days in that trench were reasonably peaceful and monotonous. In the morning, soon after sunrise, I would leave to make my report to the lieutenant and then again, shortly afterward, to supervise the distribution of supplies. We were unreasonably casual. One morning F. and I lingered outside the trenches near the path discussing a ticklish matter: we had received an extra half ration; to which of the two half platoons should it be given? I suppose that at some point we raised our voices. In any case, the Germans suddenly fired a volley of rifle shots in our direction. We fled, each to his own side. I was holding the bread and kept it.

The nights left even more vivid memories than the days. We were becoming better adapted. I now rarely ordered any firing. Nevertheless, I hardly slept. I spent long hours listening to the sounds of the forest. There was always a man on guard in the trench, ordered to inform me of the slightest alert. When he was not in his place beside me, the information he wished to give me was transmitted in a low voice from mouth to mouth. If the lookout was a bit nervous, the communications I received were occasionally bizarre. Some were weirdly precise, such as: "Sergeant, *they* are at twelve meters," when in reality *they* had not budged from their holes. On the other hand, some were terribly vague: "Sergeant, we heard a noise." When I asked, "What noise? Where?" I received no answer.

The nights were very dark. Our eyes were of no use. To avoid being surprised, we could count only on our ears. I learned to distinguish the sounds that comprise the great nocturnal murmur: the tap-tap of the raindrops on the foliage, so like the rhythm of distant footsteps, the somewhat metallic scraping sound of very dry leaves falling on the leaf-strewn forest floor (which our men so often mistook for the click of an automatic loader introduced into a German rifle breech). I could not contemplate my odd occupation there without laughing, and it was with astonishment that I realized I was matching the heroes of James Fenimore Cooper: the subtle Mohicans, or the keen trappers whom I had so admired as a child.

Things began to happen on October 17. I have mentioned that our left was covered by a trench, manned by some of the 20th company. I had visited it while establishing liaison with our neighbors. It was a pretty poor job, too shallow and much too wide. Its oocupants were at fault for not working to improve it. Having frequently been fired at by artillery, rifles, and trench mortars, they finally abandoned the position on the morning of the 19th. I realized that something serious was taking place when some panic-stricken soldiers rushed into my trench crying, "Here we are! Here we are!" I had trouble understanding what they wanted. They were men of the 20th, apparently attached to a reserve unit, who had been sent to reinforce their comrades. Having lost their way in the woods, they threw themselves into the first trench they saw. I sent them along in the right direction.

Then there was the arrival of our reserve platoon, the third, commanded at the time by Adjutant Mathon. It took up a position on our left, deployed in a skirmish line. We feared that the Germans, taking advantage of the withdrawal of the 20th, would try to disrupt our line. We had to prevent my trench from being outflanked. I helped Mathon place his men. With a single shot, Mathon, one of the best marksmen in the regiment, killed a German who, having crept stealthily through the trees, had suddenly appeared a short distance in front of us. Accompanied by a sergeant and two soldiers, Mathon went to retrieve the body. Those were our orders: staff headquarters relied heavily on the papers that we sometimes found in the enemy's pockets. Of the four-man patrol, only Mathon returned uninjured, but without the body. One soldier was killed, and the sergeant and the second soldier were both seriously wounded. Our enemies protected themselves well.

That afternoon our third platoon was replaced by one from the 24th company, sent to strengthen our battalion. A group of our new companions established themselves in the woods to the left. The rest came to reinforce us in our own trenches. Normally their leader, an adjutant, should have taken over the command that I had held up to then. By tacit agreement, however, not only the men of my own squad but all the others in the trench remained under my orders. The adjutant spent the entire time seated at the bottom of a hole, his saber between his legs and his head bowed. He lacked authority. When the commander of a trench orders a volley, presumably his chief concern is to make his men aim with care. To aim is to look, and to look is to offer one's head to enemy fire. To aim is thus dangerous. But I know only one way to persuade others to take risks, and that is to take the same risk yourself. Elementary as this truth may seem, the adjutant to whom I have referred apparently did not understand it. During the first days my men aimed too high, which was inevitable because they did not dare to raise their bodies, and too quickly, because their main purpose was to expose themselves for the least possible time. I remember having landed with all my might on one of my neighbors who, cowering in the trench with only his hand above the parapet, was brandishing his gun backward with the trigger in the air. Needless to say, I used such forceful arguments only in exceptional cases. Ordinarily I reasoned with the men, I shamed them, and with each command to fire I repeated, ''Aim low!'' Above all, at every volley I set the example by not hesitating to raise my own head. In this way my men rapidly acquired the habit of courage. The precision of their shooting saved us, as we shall see.

The night of the 17th to 18th was not bad: a few alerts, a few volleys, and that was all. Toward eight o'clock on the morning of the 18th, the Germans began to shower us furiously with big grenades from their trench mortars.

They fell with a thud and did not explode until a few
seconds after impact. As a result, we had to develop skills
to avoid them. Our observers were trained to distinguish
the noise they made on landing and to shout, "Bomb on
the right!" or "Bomb on the left!" We would throw ourselves down, shielding our heads with a knapsack or duf-
fel on the side from which the threat came. But on that
particular morning we were still inexperienced, and so in
spite of everything, it was one of those situations in which
all precautions were without effect. I was on the extreme
right of the trench. I had placed myself there because I had
hoped—unrealistically, as it proved—to be able to maintain voice communication with the corporal of the 13th
squad, who, while nominally under my orders, commanded the neighboring trench. On my left was a miner,
G., from the Pas-de-Calais, a fine lad, intelligent and
calm, who I knew could be counted on in any crisis. I was
genuinely fond of him, as he was of me. I had stationed
him beside me, first because his conversation amused me,
but even more because his acute vision reinforced my own
weak eyes. At the beginning of that appalling bombardment he had said, "This is going to be another bad day for
the 272d." I answered, "Of course not, not at all!" We
were each crouched in our own corner, with our knapsack, haversack, and canteen set up around our heads like
so many shields. It seemed to me that we had been in that
position for some time, with the shells raining all around
without hitting anyone. Then one burst with a roar on the
parapet about three meters to my left. I heard G. groan
and felt his body slump heavily on my shoulder. I could
not turn around without fully exposing myself, so I mut-
tered some words of encouragement of the sort that in-
stinctively comes to mind on such occasions: "Courage,

old man. It's nothing. Don't be afraid." Finally, taking advantage of a lull, I looked at him. When I saw his face, I stopped talking. A few minutes later he was dead. His poor body had been pierced by a fragment coming my way which had been stopped by his flesh, unquestionably saving my life. Our neighbors thought that it was I who was *in extremis*. A man of the 24th was wounded by the same blast, and gathering all his energy he attempted to leave the trench and get his wounds bound up. I tried to stop him but without success. At last the bombardment ended. I rose quickly and ordered the men to fire, fearing an attack that did not materialize. I was able to summon some men from the rear to come and get G.'s body. I helped them leave the trench. For the very first time, my arms strained under the weight of human flesh from which life had departed. Also, for the first time in this campaign, I mourned a true friend. The 24th also had a fatality. Until the morning of the 19th, he remained unburied on the rear parapet where he had been carried, his face turned toward the sun.

Through the following night we waited in vain for the attack. The day of the 19th passed without any serious incidents, though not without shrapnel and bombs. One man of the 24th suffered a slight wound in his hand when he ventured outside the trench. During the afternoon we noticed that the Germans, who were some thirty meters from us, were building a yellowish ramp. They were working lying down or on their knees; their hands were exposed for only an instant while they threw the dirt from their shovels. I ordered the men to fire, but we neither hit nor frightened them. M.,* who had taken charge of the

*Mathon.

fourth platoon, replacing the sick lieutenant, sent word that our commanding officers were expecting an attack.

At dusk, about 5 P.M., we were hit by a sudden volley of bullets. Through the clatter of rifle fire I immediately recognized the characteristic sound of those machine guns that our men had aptly named "coffee mills." One of them was extremely close. If we gave it time, it would demolish our parapet. Then its fire would force us to cower in the bottom of the trench, so that the Germans could pounce on us without warning. We had to silence it. Alas, if we had only had the weapons then that we were issued later, especially those marvelous melanite grenades! But we had only our rifles. To rid ourselves of the machine gun, we had to fire at its gunners. That was possible during the intervals in its firing, which was not continuous. But how to hit it, if we did not know its exact location? I raised myself up while it was firing and saw its flame: a big flash, redder than that of ordinary rifles. It stood there under a tree, precisely where, during the day, we had seen the yellow ramp, which I suddenly understood had been built specifically to protect this formidable weapon. The machine gun stopped. I ordered a volley, directing the fire by pointing at the target. The men aimed admirably. The machine gun resumed its spraying of our trench; and we ceased firing. Once more it stopped, and we resumed our volleys. And so on. After a little time, the Germans repositioned their gun, and the same old game continued. How long, altogether, did it last? I do not know; but I do know that the machine gun was finally silenced. We no longer heard it; and at almost the same moment, the German rifles fell silent. M. sent us his congratulations as well as those of the captain.

The Germans had not, however, given up hope of wip-

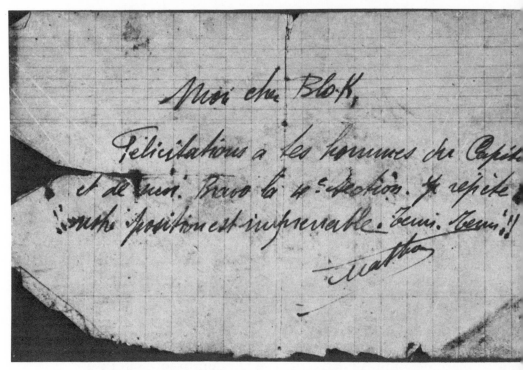

Note from Mathon to Bloch: "Mon cher Blok [sic], Félicitations à les hommes du Capitaine et de moi. Bravo la 4ᵉ Section. Je répète: notre position est imprenable Tenir. Tenir!! Mathon" (My dear Bloch, Congratulations to the men from the captain and from me. Bravo, 4th Section. I repeat: our position is impregnable. Hold on, hold on!! Mathon).

ing out our position. During the night they attacked us three times. What a racket! They left their trenches; we heard them coming, but we never saw them. Our shots stopped them each time. I directed the fire standing up, scanning the woods to judge its effect. I had rolled up my blanket around my chin as a sort of protective collar. Only my eyes showed from under my kepi; and I folded a scarf over my face in the no doubt mistaken hope that it would diminish the force of any hit. I had placed myself near the middle of the trench. My two neighbors, a corporal of the 24th company, very brave and self-possessed, and a soldier from my platoon, both pulled my cloak to force me back down. I said, "You're very kind, but leave me alone!" The third attack found me asleep, having succumbed to my fatigue in spite of myself. Someone woke me with "Sergeant, sergeant!" and I rose just in time to shout, "Fire at will at the brush in front. Fire hard! Fire hard!"

In the morning we were finally relieved under a hail of bullets. One man lost his way in the woods. We never saw him again. What a relief, when we were finally out of La Gruerie, to see the sun shining on the meadows of La Harazée! I learned that there were three wounded in the third squad and two in the second half platoon. We returned, exhausted, parched, and lightheaded, to La Neuville-au-Pont. During a halt on the side of the road where it turns off from Vienne-le-Château, the captain came and congratulated me, telling my men that they could follow me under fire with confidence, and added that I was a real *poilu*. I answered that my beard, now full grown and wholly unkempt, justified the epithet.

IV

From October 20th through the 27th we rested, first at La Neuville-au-Pont and then at Florent, in the "mo-

notonous quiet of the camp," according to my journal. Having left Florent in the middle of the afternoon of
the 27th, we spent the night in shelters on the edge of a
wood near La Placardelle. On the 28th, shortly after dawn,
we reentered La Gruerie, where our battalion was placed
to the right of its former position.

This new sojourn in the heart of the forest lasted until
the morning of November 3. Most of my comrades in the
272d would have been astonished to hear that it left me
with a pleasant memory. For several of our companies it
was marred by bloody episodes. In my own company at
least two platoons were sorely tested. Yet in the fourth
platoon we passed some reasonably agreeable days. The
Germans, who were not far off but whom we never saw,
did not disturb our peace. They fired from time to time,
especially at night. One of them, no doubt a tenacious and
methodical soul, aimed always in the same direction,
slightly to the right of my trench. He never caused us any
harm, but his stubbornness was infuriating. We called him
"the little stinker over there." From time to time we heard
someone in the shadows shouting, "Feu-er!" dragging out
the dipthong like an officer commanding several hundred
men. This naive bluff did not bother us. It did not take us
long to notice that each time a dozen rifles at most carried
out the order given in this exaggerated manner. Toward
the end of our stay, a few bombs were aimed directly at us.
A good number never exploded. They were propelled
slowly, and we saw them rise in the night sky, where they
described beautiful arcs of reddish light. The first fell not
far from me and, after the explosion, released a malodor-
ous gas that we found extremely disagreeable. We were
not in one continuous trench, but quartered by twos or
threes in underground shelters connected by long, narrow

paths. To share my shelter I had chosen a miner from the Pas-de-Calais and a Parisian worker, two good fellows with whom I got along well. Together we managed a comfortable little mess. I have never eaten finer buttered toast than in that forsaken hole in the woods. During the day I would go out to direct the distribution of supplies or to deliver my report to the platoon leader, to make the rounds, to keep in touch with my neighbors, or on any other pretext, when I became bored with my lair. At night we took turns as lookout. This vigil, ordinarily uneventful, seemed endless. I struggled with difficulty against my drowsiness; and I remember some lovely glimpses of the moon between the branches.

On the morning of November 3 we returned to La Neuville-au-Pont. We remained there, at rest, until the evening of the 8th. Second Lieutenant A., up to then leader of the fourth platoon, in which I had served under his orders, left for a battalion of engineers that had recently been formed. Very young—he was just twenty five—he was a pleasant companion, very simple and reliable. I missed him. I took over his command with the rank of adjutant. The captain and his platoon leaders had a common mess. Till then I had almost always eaten with my men and shared their life. Now I left them. This was a great change. Henceforth I had a few of those comforts that, though indeed modest, seem precious at the front, especially during bad weather. I am speaking not only of purely material things—more nourishing and more plentiful food, more carefully served, and quarters more conducive to rest; these were no trivial advantages, and only an idiot would turn up his nose at them. But they are not the best. A table, a lamp (oh, how I had suffered without one during the first autumn evenings, which had seemed so long in our quarters!), a quiet corner where I could read, write, or merely think or dream; these are the talismans that make life more agreeable and cheerful in wartime. Add to these the pleasure of more polished conversation, the company of a more subtle and intelligent conversationalist such as our captain, and more opportunity for news and of knowing what was going on in the regiment and in the world. Naturally I welcomed with pleasure all these comforts that my promotion brought me. But I do not regret having begun at a more humble rank, which placed me in closer contact with the men. Having been thus thrown in among my troops, I came to know them better.

From November 8 to 15 we were again on the front line in the woods above Four-de-Paris. My platoon was broken up. I chose to remain with the second half platoon on the slope of a ravine at the bottom of which the Germans had established a small post. Our trench blocked a path that followed the side of the slope and led to the enemy's positions, a few hundred meters away. I was poorly situated in a narrow ditch. The hours we passed there were quiet and dull. Two false alerts, some harmless shrapnel, the misadventure of a soldier on patrol who, for venturing contrary to my orders toward the left side of the road in full view of the enemy, had his cheek ripped open by a bullet, and my own fall into a muddy stream when returning at night—these are all that my memory has retained of unusual happenings that enlivened our peaceful outing.

On the 15th we were relieved by colonials, if I remember correctly. Here, at this relief, my journal ends. I had never written in it day by day, yet up till then I had always tried to keep it up to date. After November 16 I wrote nothing more. The wound I received at the end of November, slight but nevertheless annoying, then the onset of the illness that announced itself by a dull weariness and by more and more frequent indisposition help explain my laziness, which I regret today. Yet even without the aid of my journal, I can still bring back memories that have remained quite clear, although I cannot date them.

After another rest in La Neuville-au-Pont, we left once more for La Gruerie. As usual the relief took place at night. The cold was penetrating. The puddles of water in the woods were frozen. An incredibly slick coating of ice covered the footpaths, which in some places were very steep. We could make our way only with great difficulty and with frequent tumbles. We did not arrive until day-break.

Our line, which had gradually been improved, no longer contained the gaps that had made life so difficult in the past. My platoon, now stationed on the right of the company, was able to communicate easily under cover with the two adjoining platoons. Our trench had an absurd shape. On the left was a series of shelters; on the right, a long crenellated passage describing a curve whose concave side faced the enemy; in the center, an outpost that could be only half occupied, the right side having virtually collapsed; and connecting all of that, a network of passages that spread out toward the rear. Once the men were settled and provisional orders given, our first concern was to reconnoiter the surrounding area. Under the gray light of dawn, I discovered a remarkable landscape. One would not have believed we were in a forest. The shells and even more the machine gun fire had mowed down the branches and even the trunks of trees. On our right, toward the rear, a large oak had been cut down; the trunk was still connected with the stump by only a few fibers, and its top rested on the ground. In front, a yellowish knoll had been formed by the debris of a collapsed, abandoned shelter. Next to it a corpse in a French great-coat lay face down. Farther on (though still quite close) I saw a long, pale brown slope on which were some sandbags and here and there some metal plates pierced by rectangular openings. These were the German trenches. On the left they veered away from us, running slantwise, across a clearing from which we were separated by 30 or 40 meters. On our right they formed a salient that continued opposite the trenches of the 17th company, our neighbors. I estimated a distance of twelve meters between our parapet and the closest German rampart.

Our stay there lasted three or four days. There is something frightening in feeling that close to the enemy. One leap, and they would be in our midst. Moreover, I had no confidence in the trenches. At night, everyone remained on watch, with fixed bayonet. I made the rounds frequently. During the day, a third of the men remained on watch; another third was employed in the eternal task of excavation, which was always necessary in a trench; and a third slept. We hardly ever heard the Germans. Like us, they had become accustomed to talking softly. There were only the sounds of shovels, picks, or hatchets, which could not very well be muffled. It was very cold. We lit some fires: at such short distance, we no longer feared being seen. I had a fine shelter, with a bed of beaten earth and a hearth, which unfortunately smoked. A narrow window provided light and allowed me to look around; but unfortunately it exposed anyone lying down to a direct hit. One of my predecessors had been wounded that way. But what could one do? I found in this dwelling a red eiderdown quilt, which kept my feet warm, and also an anthology with many pages missing; in its present condi-

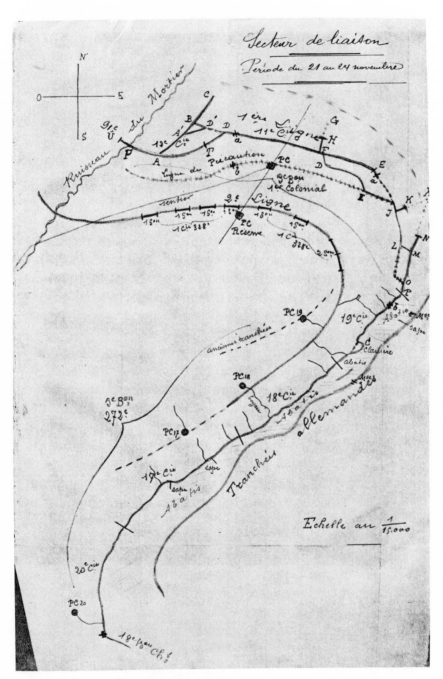

272d Regiment map: French and German emplacements at La Gruerie,
November 21–24, 1914

tion it began with a "Sermon on Death," which I did not read.

Opposite us, some superb marksmen lay in wait. The first day, at dawn, as I raised myself slightly on the parapet of the most forward part of the trench to reconnoiter our position, I heard the sound of a breech block. I jumped to the ground as a bullet whistled overhead. Our opponents were completely self-possessed. On one occasion I had someone throw a melanite grenade, which fell short at the foot of the enemy embankment, apparently wounding no one but exploding with enough noise and smoke to frighten the most steadfast; the black cloud had hardly cleared before the German soldier in the observation post, at the point of the trench at which we had aimed and missed, fired precisely in the direction from where our projectile had been launched.

For a unit taking up a position very close to the enemy, the most dangerous hours are always those immediately following its arrival. The men need time to acquire the habit of extreme caution that such situations demand. On our first morning we were cruelly tested. We had two dead and one wounded: all three hit by bullets in the head. When a bullet strikes the skull at a certain angle, it explodes. That was the way L. died. I went to bring him back. Half his face hung like a shutter whose hinges no longer held, and one could see inside the almost empty cranial box. I covered the horrible wound with a handkerchief to keep it hidden from my men. Peasants and workers, whom one expects to be uncouth, are often remarkably sensitive. I myself am able to withstand bloody sights without too much distress. I knew that L. had died without suffering; indeed, it was less terrible to see his poor head than later to find the photograph of his two small sons in his wallet.

If the Germans thus made things difficult for us, we for our part did not remain inactive. I tried to use the grenade thrower that a Captain C. had just invented. A brigadier of artillery in charge of testing it was scouring our trenches, his minuscule cannon under his arm, offering his services to all the platoon leaders. An affable individual, he modestly praised his merchandise. I accepted his proposals; but either because the machine had not yet been perfected or more likely because my trench, given its shape and its location in the middle of a forest, where despite everything there were still some trees, was badly suited to the purpose, we obtained only mediocre results. The gunner fired two grenades. Both struck branches and the second all but fell back on our own heads. That ended the experiment. Our principal weapon remained the melanite grenades that were thrown by hand after the cap was lit. I had a great thrower in T., a mine worker who was endowed with a strong arm and imperturbable courage. Before lighting the wick, he would cut it so close that I always expected to see the melanite explode in his hands. Thanks to this daring, the grenades would explode the moment they landed, thus giving the enemy no time to escape. Once I threw one at a group of workers I had heard digging. The explosion was followed by frightful cries, so near that my men thought T. or I had been wounded. Although we had become terribly hardened, my blood froze, and I saw that T. had turned white. This is not one of my better memories.

We were too near our adversaries not to be tempted to communicate with them. I wrote them a sort of proclamation. We had been told that there were some Poles among them, so I invited them to desert. I intended to add some French newspapers to my parcel. While I was preparing my packet, my attention was diverted somehow to a small group that was working at the bottom of the clearing just opposite me. We could not see them, but the sound of their tools and especially the movement of the trees, whose lower branches they were no doubt removing, revealed their presence. I went to the forward trench and called for a salvo in their direction. Exactly at the moment I ordered "Fire!" I received a heavy blow on the forehead above my left eye; I fell on my knees, crying, "I've been hit!" A bullet had struck the rifle of a man who was shooting in front of me, and had caused its magazine to explode. I had been hit either by the splinters of the German bullet, which had perhaps been specially prepared to fragment on contact, or by the explosion of the French bullets in the magazine. I say the splinters because in addition to the wound next to my eyebrow I had some scratches on my cheek and in my hair, and my kepi was pierced in a number of places. I had read that mortal blows are often not very painful, and I also knew that head wounds are ordinarily either very serious or insignificant. I thought, "If I'm not dead in two minutes, I'll be all right." Having survived the two fatal minutes, I judged that all would be well. I prepared an improvised dressing for my wounds and left to find the medical officer.

On the way I came upon the battalion commander at his post. He made a detailed inquiry into the circumstances of my misadventure and the condition of my trench, reproaching me with due severity for the indisputable imprudence of having raised my head. Then, abruptly changing his tone, he urged that I take good care of my-

La Gruerie: first-aid station

self. As I made my way down toward La Harazée, where the field hospital was located, he ran after me to advise me to take the "low road," since the "high road" was exposed to rifle fire. At La Harazée I was examined and bandaged. The medical officer predicted that I would have a black eye. His prophesy proved all too accurate. During the next days, my eye, both by its shape and by its color, was a source of amazement and delight to my entourage; but I easily obtained permission to return to the trenches. I resumed my command and was offered some warm wine in honor of the occasion; but I never sent either my proclamation or my newspapers. That night a platoon of chasseurs came to replace us. I was drowsing when my dispatch runner announced their arrival. I had difficulty opening my eyes.

V

That time we did not go to La Neuville-au-Pont, which we were never to see again. We were sent to Vienne-le-Château. Later, during December, we spent two days at Chaudefontaine, near Ste-Menehould. Until the end of my months in the field, with the exception of those two days, Vienne-le-Château remained the place we rested each time we returned from the trenches. A most illusory rest! The necessary chores—especially washing my muddy belongings—and guard duty at the approaches to our camp or in support of the neighboring batteries would take up most or our days.

Vienne-le-Château was built on both banks of the Biesme, which turned its water mills. Despite its comfortable air, the village itself was in no way remarkable. When I knew it, however, it lay within range of German artillery, and the shells had given it an unnaturally picturesque air.

Vienne-le-Château: church

With its crumbling walls, its houses ripped apart, exposing their ruined interiors through gaping facades, its smoking debris, and its steeple with the top blown off, it was Arras or Rheims in miniature. Altogether, the shells caused more noise than actual damage. Many of the houses were still standing, and only once did I see people injured. There is nothing one becomes accustomed to more easily than a bombardment. This explains the heroism of so many cities under siege. I doubt that either shrapnel or high-explosive shells ever prevented us from sleeping or taking walks or, if we had the opportunity, from amusing ourselves. Nevertheless, we would have preferred to rest farther from the front. We did not mind the roar of the cannon, but to hear the whistling of shells even in our quarters seemed excessive. That music should have been reserved for the trenches.

The château from which Vienne had taken its name once stood on a hill almost completely surrounded by houses. Nothing remained now but the cellars, which were built on several levels and were very large. We spent a night in them, and I think it was there that I caught the bronchitis from which I was suffering when I came down with typhoid. Usually we were quartered in the "shacks," situated on the slope of a pine-covered hill at the entrance of the village. The officers stayed in houses "in town." It was also "in town" that we had our mess; and during my last stay, I too slept in a room, and even a bed. Our staff headquarters had ordered the civilian population to leave. We slept in their beds, ate at their tables on their linen, with the light of their lamps, often consuming their provisions. It was the life of brigands. In spite of the military police, there was a lot of looting. Many an armchair found its way into the huts or even into the trenches. We took

Vienne-leChâteau: effects of bombardment

Vienne-le-Château: village and watering place

bell jars from the gardens to light our cabins and stoves from the houses to heat them. I have on my conscience the theft of a candlestick and a collection of poems edited around 1830. I lost the candlestick, but I still have the book. Vienne-le-Château had a felt factory, whose principal product was a beautiful red fez. That fez became the men's favorite headdress during their days off.

Vienne-le-Château evokes an exceedingly painful memory. One morning during our third stay, shortly before sunrise, I was awakened by cries for help. One of our huts, the one occupied by the second half platoon, had collapsed. Still half asleep, I failed at first to grasp the enormity of the situation. I ran toward the scene of the disaster and finally understood. The rains had gradually eroded the soil of the small slope. The clayish mass that formed the rear of the hut (which, like most of the others, had been set in a cavity dug directly into the hill) suddenly separated itself from the adjoining ground and began crushing the frail, virtually unsupported structure. Under a heap of tangled beams, branches, and clods of mud, the wounded groaned and cried for help. We worked to free them. It was difficult to see. The first flickers of daylight had hardly begun to penetrate the darkness. For light we had only a few flashlights and candles, which the wind extinguished. It was already too late to save all our comrades. Out of the ruins we recovered not only seven wounded, including some seriously injured, but also, alas, three bodies. My good friend F. was among the dead. It was only after a long struggle that we were able to recover his body. By then it was already daylight. His pale face emerged, hardly dirty, with his huge black eyes wide open. In the afternoon we buried the pathetic victims of this absurd accident. I realized that they too, in their fashion, had fallen on the field of honor. Still, I would have felt less grief if they had succumbed to the enemy. The captain was to speak at the cemetery, but he was so moved that after pronouncing a few words he had to stop.

At Vienne-le-Château we had one day of great happiness, quickly over. It was about December 20. Toward midnight I was awakened by Captain Q., a staff officer, who had returned from seeing the colonel. He told me that the battalion would be leaving before dawn, around 4 A.M., I believe. This was unprecedented: we were in the middle of a rest period. Q. added: "It's the big attack." In the morning we occupied the second line of trenches between Vienne and La Harazée. There we received the order of the day from General Joffre, announcing the offensive destined to liberate the country once and for all. I found the text, which I read to my men, deeply moving. And how pleased they were! Trench warfare had become so slow, so dreary, so debilitating to body and soul that even the least brave among us wholeheartedly welcomed the prospect of an attack. Our cannon roared throughout the day. The enemy's artillery responded weakly. That evening the captain and I, seated on the threshold of our common shelter, watched the distant flashes in the east beyond the Argonne, which we assumed to be a violent battle. Then the company was ordered back to Vienne, and there was no further talk of an offensive.

Ordinarily we left Vienne-le-Château only to return to the front line. The two battalions of the regiment relieved each other on an average of every seven days. We always occupied the same sector, in open country, on the clay plateau that stretched between the woods of La Gruerie on the east and the valley of the Aisne on the west. Our company was invariably placed on the left of the battalion,

Vienne-le-Château: column returning to the trenches

which itself was pushed farther to the left by the colonials. Little by little we edged our trenches forward from the side of the wood toward the road from Servon to Vienne-le-Château. By the end of December we reached the road. From there we could see a broad horizon. In front of us, just beyond the slope where the lines of the enemy trenches became clearly visible against the darker surrounding soil, we could see the belfry of Binarville pointing to the sky. When we wanted to speak of a great struggle or a brilliant offensive, we would not say, "When we are at Mézieres" or "at Lille," but "When we are at Binarville." I believe that we are not there yet.

If I were to divide my combat experience into periods, I would name this last the "age of mud." It rained frequently. The water could neither seep down nor run off on this impermeable, almost flat terrain. Our trenches served as its channels. After every downpour we emptied the water. And opposite us the Germans had to do the same, which gave us some small consolation. The walls of the trenches caved in. It was constantly necessary to consolidate, to clear away, to board over and dig again. Our men were exhausted by these incessant labors. The clay stuck to their spades and became glued to their hands. Once my shelter, which had been weakened by the rains, collapsed. Fortunately I had realized it was disintegrating and had taken the precaution of moving out. The weather was never very cold. But the unrelieved dampness was even harder to bear than frigid temperatures would have been. Our clothing was completely soaked for days on end. Our feet were chilled. The sticky clay clung to our shoes, our clothing, our underwear, our skin; it spoiled our food, threatened to plug the barrels of our rifles and to jam their breeches. Returning to the line was always painful. It al-

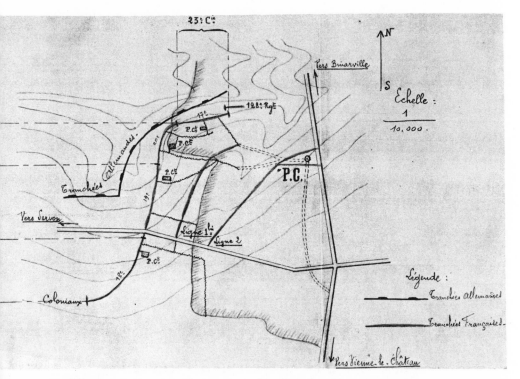

272d Regiment map: emplacements at La Gruerie, December 4, 1914

153

ways took place at night and usually when it was very dark. We slid on the water-soaked ground. The shell holes and the abandoned trenches, only half filled by cave-ins, became so many hidden hazards in the shadows. We always returned to Vienne-le-Château exhausted and grumbling, covered from head to foot with a crust of dirt. Yet even in this muddy inferno, there were the rare good moments.

We were not particularly exposed. Shells whistled incessantly over our heads because a French battery behind us frequently exchanged fire with the Germans; but most of the projectiles were not aimed at us. Our gunners, however, had a mad passion for dropping occasional short shots, with the result that they sometimes hit us instead of the enemy emplacements. On January 4 they killed or wounded a few men in the first platoon in this way. Sometimes we were bombarded by the Germans. Their shells never hit anyone in my platoon. On the side of the road to Servon there was a small, very low building, which we could barely see from our lines. The artillery officers insisted that it covered either a machine gun nest or the entrance to a German tunnel. Actually it was only the cabin of a road worker, as two night patrols that I dispatched there confirmed. An officer of the neighboring battery who came to our trenches refused to admit his comrades' error. Irritated, I resolved to undertake my own reconnaissance of the miserable cabin, so I might personally verify the testimony of my men. On the way there, I easily eluded the enemy's view; but on my return, when I had crept up a small incline to observe their trenches, I was finally spotted. They saluted me with rifle shots. I had to get back to our lines by crawling on my stomach. There was no danger; the riflemen barely saw me. Nevertheless,

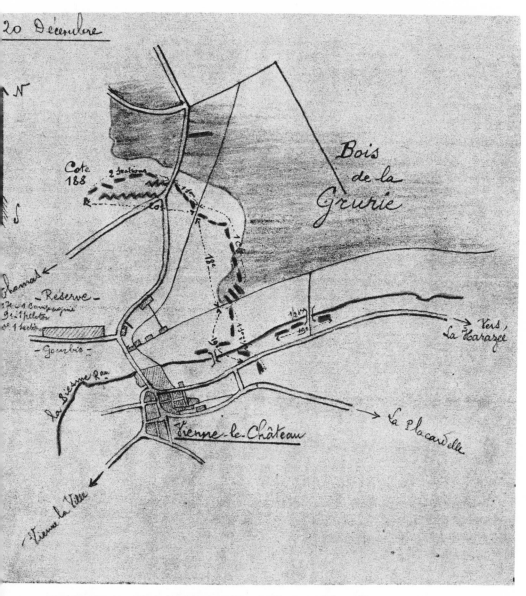

272d Regiment map: emplacements at La Gruerie, December 20, 1914

I suffered acutely that particular feeling shared by all who
have ever been shot at: exasperation combined with un-
easiness, as when during a social gathering one is cor-
nered by a crank.

When dusk fell, we often left our lairs, either to see the
captain, who stayed in the rear with the reserve platoon,
or to visit among ourselves. Protected by the irregular terrain, we were rarely bothered by stray bullets. One evening, when the leaders of the three front-line platoons
were thus meeting with the captain (undoubtedly because
we wanted to borrow his newspapers), firing suddenly
broke out at the front. We had to race like fools to get back
to our posts. After that, the three of us avoided absenting
ourselves at the same time. On Christmas eve, in the captain's shelter, I met my schoolmate and colleague from
Amiens, B., who, as second lieutenant of the 72d, had
come with his platoon to reinforce our company. The captain had received a bottle of champagne. We drank to
victory. I was never to see B. again. He was killed on
March 3, during the assault on Beauséjour.

In these trenches my platoon lost three men. Two were
killed by bullets: one returning at daybreak from a search
party for wood, which I blame myself for having sent out
too late, the other hit in the head by a stray shot. The third
was the victim of our medical officers. He was a Breton
territorial named G. Our regiment, reduced more by illness than by combat, had been restored to full strength
toward the middle of December by territorials who arrived
from depots in Brittany. Among them were a few naval
recruits who made good soldiers. But the others who came
from the interior struck us as indifferent warriors. Prematurely aged, they seemed depressed by both poverty and
alcohol. Their ignorance of the language made them seem

all the more brutish. To compound this misfortune, they had been recruited from the four corners of Brittany so that each spoke a different dialect, and those among them who knew some French could rarely serve as interpreters for the others. G. was one of the least enlightened. Gentle and resigned as most of them were, but incapable of understanding or being understood, he seemed to live in another world. His appearance was pathetic: small, thin, and extremely pale. Toward the end of December, he seemed to feel ill. We were then in the trenches. Every morning before dawn, the battalion doctors made their rounds at the command post. G. went there two days in a row without being noticed. On the second day, on his way back to the trench, he fainted. I told him to go back again the following day and give him a note that at my request the captain had written to the doctors, stressing the urgency of his case. It was never delivered. That same day, about nine o'clock in the evening, G. died. We buried him that night behind the trenches.

We spent New Year's Day at Vienne-le-Château; then during the night of January 2–3 we returned to the front line. For some time I had felt decidedly ill, and all my efforts to master the ailment had failed. The evening of the third I decided to ask the captain for authorization to return to the base camp. He readily agreed, indeed he urged me to go. A soldier who was being sent to Vienne-le-Château to pick up mail went with me. He kindly carried my sack, but not being as brave as he was obliging, he forced me along at a furious pace where the road was exposed to shellfire. Out of breath, my head already heavy, I was barely able to keep up with him. I fell two or three times. On the morning of the fifth, the medical officer evacuated me to Ste-Menehould. From the automobile

Evacuation of wounded from La Harazée, 1915

that carried me toward the rear, I could hear the familiar roll of the cannon fading little by little into the distance.

VI

Thus from August 10, 1914, to January 5, 1915, I led a life as different as possible from my ordinary existence: a life at once barbarous, violent, often colorful, also often of a dreary monotony combined with bits of comedy and moments of grim tragedy. In five months in the field, who would not have amassed a rich harvest of experiences?

Like everyone else, I was impressed by the total inadequacy of our material preparation as well as of our military training. In La Gruerie I installed wire without barbs. I have seen my trench showered with bombs to which we could respond only with rifle fire. I have ordered the ground dug with hand tools and intrigued with my colleagues to secure a few good full-size implements for my platoon. I saw—alas, right up to the end—the inadequacy of our telephone lines impede our communication with the artillery. Moreover, only experience taught me—and no doubt most imperfectly—how to dig trenches. Reflecting later on what we did during the first months of war, I realized that the corps of engineers knew little more about that problem than we did. Before Larzicourt, didn't our officers build for our battalion commander a shelter that was cleverly hidden in a cabbage field but totally lacking any direct communication with the front lines? Thus, in the event of an attack, our unhappy major, after having killed off all his quartermaster sergeants by sending them with his orders to the various companies, would have been forced to watch, like a powerless spectator, the combat he should have been directing. I saw progress occur slowly, with difficulty, but surely. By December we had

159

Developed trenchwork in the Argonne, July 1915

more barbed wire and pointed stakes than we knew what to do with. I heard the noise of our artillery, so weak and intermittent during our first stay in La Gruerie, grow gradually to dominate the uproar of the enemy's cannon.

I was aware, especially at the start of the campaign, of some shocking negligence. When we were holding the trenches near Thonne-la-Long we had absolutely no idea what was in front of us. One day, when we thought we had made contact with the enemy, the French outposts were still in front of us. Our orders to leave Han-les-Juvigny arrived several hours late. At Larzicourt we worked under the supervision of the corps of engineers. On the first day we exerted considerable effort to dig trenches that, being visible from a distance, would have offered the enemy's artillery an invaluable target. The next day the engineers' captain, who was billeted in the village, examined our work, correctly judged it unacceptable, and made us start again; had he come the day before to direct our inexperienced efforts, he could have spared us both the painful fatigue and the discouragement of our wasted efforts. One of my men, a master carpenter from a town in the Ile-de-France, said, "If I were responsible for work like that, I'd soon have to close up shop." Wasn't he right?

I was by no means always satisfied with our officers. Often I found them insufficiently concerned with their men's well-being, too ignorant of their physical condition, and too uninterested to find out. The words "Let them cope"—that sinister phrase which, after 1870, no one should have dared utter again—were still too often on their lips. The officers' and platoon leaders' mess sometimes appropriated too large a share of the supplies. The officers' cooks played too important a role in the company. The quartermaster sergeants should have been kept under closer scrutiny. Obviously there may have been regiments to which my criticisms do not apply. I can only speak of what I have seen, and the range of my experience was necessarily very limited. When in quarters, the company officers did not assemble their men frequently enough. Reservists are no longer children; they always impressed me as eager for news, and its lack discouraged them. It was up to their officers to keep them informed of developments and to comment on them. I had a captain who understood admirably how to communicate with his troops; why didn't he do it more often? In fairness, I should add that at Vienne-le-Château we were forced to avoid meetings, which would be dangerous in a village under constant bombardment.

Our battalion, and then the sixth, were for the time commanded by a captain who was a coarse and contemptible individual. He knew only two ways to make his men perform: either by insulting them or by threatening them with a court-martial. I heard him vilify some men who two days earlier (September 10) had stood without flinching under the devastating cannon and machine gun fire that had covered the German retreat. Once he hit someone; but I believe that incident was hushed up. Our revenge was to watch the terrible fright that his features betrayed at the sound of shellfire. Promoted major, he had himself recalled on the pretext of general exhaustion, which no one believed. But my battalion also served under an officer whom I greatly admired. With a somewhat severe appearance as well as a brusque manner and speech, his thin, almost ascetic face revealed no trace of humor. Yet, though he made not the slightest effort to be popular, he possessed that mysterious quality of personal magnetism which transforms a man into a leader; his soldiers had faith in him and would have followed him anywhere. In my comrade M., a reenlisted noncommissioned officer who rose to second lieutenant, I found the charm of simple courage along with the happy combination of cool self-possession and personal warmth. It was he who produced the heroic reply—so much finer because of its obvious innocence of any literary pretension—when a panic-stricken soldier cried, "The Germans are only thirty meters away from us," "Well, we are only thirty meters away from the Germans."

A company or platoon is not made up of men equally intelligent, attractive, or brave. When I recall the comrades with whom I have lived, men I have commanded, the figures I evoke do not all seem pleasant. By knowing Corporal H., I learned just how far malingering could go (how far in this case would probably have been a court-martial if the lieutenant had not been so kind, perhaps too kind). When I remember the face of Corporal M., I cannot restrain a smile. He was a miner, stocky and rather heavy-footed, with a square face; his nose was adorned with a fine blueish scar of the sort that the carbon dust of the coal pit frequently imprints on workers' bodies. Though an indefatigable walker, he was unaccustomed to shoes, so he traveled the roads of Lorraine and Champagne barefoot. He was so careless and so stupid that it now seems to me I did little during the first six weeks of the campaign but hunt for him from one end of the camp to the other, to transmit orders he never understood. But I should not forget that the last thing I did not succeed in making him understand, on the morning of September 10, was that his place was not at the head of the platoon. When we went into action that day, he fell, whether killed or wounded I do not know.

During the month of August and the first days of September, D. was our joy. A peasant from the region of Baupaume, he had the most beautiful Picard accent. When we saw the first wounded along the route between Grand-Verneuil and Thonne-la-Long, we noticed that many had their arms in slings, leaving their unused coat sleeves dangling. D. thought they were all amputees, and we were never able to convince him that he was mistaken. Very coarse in his own language, he accepted the grossest insults from his comrades without flinching; only one expression infuriated him: "Shut your _____." He absolutely insisted on having a "mouth." I also muse over our handful of cowards: K., who all but spat at me when I happened on him by chance in his shelter; V., who, miserable at finding himself at war, never referred to himself without saying, "Poor martyr!" But I prefer to remember the good chaps: P., of whose death I have just learned, a Parisian worker with pale complexion, who had the insatiable appetite of a man who has not had all he wanted to eat, who has frequently gone hungry, and who was restless, nervous, and quick both to anger and to rejoice; poor G., secretary of a miners' union, active and talkative, and with a truly generous heart; and T., also a miner, uneducated, as taciturn as G. was loquacious, of dark complexion and gloomy expression, calm in moments of danger and burning with an unquenchable hatred of Germans, whom he never referred to except as "those assassins." Who will ever record the unknown acts of heroism performed in La Gruerie by our dispatch runners? I can still see our first, T., by occupation a manual laborer from Pontoise, small and quick, full of pompous phrases. He trotted through the wood, which was being sprayed with bursts of fire;

and when a bullet passed too close, he made with his hand the gesture one uses to chase away a bothersome fly.

Of all my comrades who fell in Champagne or in the Argonne, there is none I mourned more than F., who was the sergeant of my second half platoon. F.'s line of work was not one usually considered important. He ran a shop for a wine merchant near the Bastille. He had scant education and could barely read. Yet no one has done more to make me understand the beauty of a truly noble and sensitive soul. He rarely used coarse language, and I never heard him utter an obscenity. His men adored him for his kindly good nature, which rubbed off on them. His calm courage inspired their confidence because they knew he was prudent as well as brave. Remarkably attentive to the practical details of life, he was one of those of whom it was said he always knew which way was north. I still remember his return from one dangerous patrol he had undertaken with resolute courage, confiding his wallet to me as he left, and which he led with a truly remarkable equanimity. He came back carrying a can of food that he had found in an abandoned sack somewhere between the lines. He devoted himself to making life more agreeable for those of his men he thought were poor, and shared with them those small treats that are beyond price in the field. He had a lofty notion of loyalty among comrades, which he explained by saying, "When I was a recruit, I was in a squad where we got along well together." Unquestionably his main desire and his greatest effort was to ensure that his half platoon should "get along well together." When I lost him, I lost a moral support.

During my months in the field I sometimes saw men show fear. The look of fear I found very ugly. To be sure, I encountered it very seldom. Military courage is certainly widespread. I do not believe it is correct to say, despite occasional opinions to the contrary, that it is easily come by. Not always, to be fair, but often it is the result of effort, an effort that a healthy individual makes without injury to himself and which rapidly becomes instinctive. I have always noticed that by some fortunate reflex, death ceases to appear very terrible the moment it seems close: it is this, ultimately, that explains courage. Most men dread going under fire, and especially returning to it. Once there, however, they no longer tremble. Also, I believe that few soldiers, except the most noble or intelligent, think of their country while conducting themselves bravely; they are much more often guided by a sense of personal honor, which is very strong when it is reinforced by the group. If a unit consisted of a majority of slackers, the point of honor would be to get out of any situation with the least harm possible. Thus I always thought it a good policy to express openly the profound disgust that the few cowards in my platoon inspired in me.

I have finished gathering my memories. T., of whom I have just spoken, wrote me a letter the other day; because it is in pencil, it will no doubt soon fade away. In order not to forget his last sentence, I shall copy it here: "Vive la France, et vivement la victoire!" ("Long live France, and let victory come quickly!").

PART II

Almost two years ago, during a convalescent leave, I began to assemble my memories of the war. Today I shall take up the task again. The accidents of war have provided me with some unanticipated leisure. The 250th brigade (to which my regiment, the 72d, belongs) has had an unusual adventure. The conscription of native soldiers in Algeria having provoked some difficulties, especially in the province of Constantine, the governor general became upset, feared the worst, and called for the army. We had barely emerged from the fierce fighting of the Somme, in which we had suffered serious losses, when we were assigned to Algeria. In this beautiful climate we have now settled into most peaceful winter quarters. For my part, I lead a quiet life in Constantine, comfortable though somewhat empty. The moment has come to call on the past to fill up the present.

I

Return to the front, July 13, 1915

On June 7, 1915, at the end of my convalescent leave, I rejoined the depot of the 72d and 272d infantry regiments at Morlaix. I stayed only a few days. I was not at all comfortable there. At the time I wrote a friend, "I am leaving the depot for fear of losing my morale, which I value above all." In these depots, one meets a group of soldiers and even officers who cling desperately to the dreary but safe existence characteristic of a small garrison town in the rear. In order to remain there as long as possible, they are capable, if not of evil actions, at least of a host of mean little maneuvers. Though at heart good souls who behave honorably and at times display an amazing heroism once they are thrown into the furnace, they are weak spirits who panic at the anticipation of far-off danger. Exposure to this kind of funk brings out one's own courage. I felt well again, and I burned to be useful. Besides, I have never liked to wait: if danger must come, I prefer to face it at once. Some reinforcements were leaving to join the 72d, and I signed up as a volunteer. On June 22 I left Morlaix. My parents and sister-in-law came to see me off. By mutual agreement, we avoided any excess sentiment.

Troop trains are not fast. Avoiding direct routes, they amble slowly along winding secondary lines. The soldiers, crowded against the doors, sing of the virtue of stationmasters' wives. To get from Morlaix to the front took us three days and four nights. When I try to recall those endless days, three or four pictures come to mind: Angers, white under the morning sun, and the warm welcome of the Louises; the Loire valley, which we followed for hours, the river almost motionless, its banks of golden sand, the cottonwoods, the hills, and the peaceful, lazy landscape that presented to my view everything to which I had said *au revoir*, and perhaps *adieu;* awakening early in the morning at Le Creusot, its factories crowded between dreary hills, smoke streaking the sky with gray, and along the dirty streets workers hurrying to their jobs, wearing the mobilization armband on their sleeves: already marked for war.

At Is-sur-Tille we ran into an eccentric stationmaster. This small, angry man, dressed in khaki, displayed a ferocious passion for what he liked to call "the discipline of the front." In fact, he mercilessly harassed the troops who passed through his station on their way to the firing line, where he himself had never been. Thus he forbade the station guards to mail letters for our men, who, not being allowed to leave the platform, could not put them in the box themselves. This led to a host of small incidents, and finally to the arrest of one of our officers who had protested too vigorously.

The *Cri de Paris* related the story of a stationmaster who, rightly or wrongly believing that he had been insulted by two chasseur lieutenants, took their names and the numbers of their battalions and filed charges. His superintendent welcomed the action and demanded punishment for the two offenders, claiming further that the stationmaster's job was a thankless one and it was therefore necessary to avoid discouraging these men. Unfortunately, the numbers had been misread or poorly transcribed, an error that naturally delayed the procedure. When the complaint was presented to the sixth chasseur brigade, commanded by Colonel M., and the accused officers were finally identified, the attack launched by the chasseurs in the woods of St-Vaast on November 7, 1916, had already taken place. More than forty officers fell during this action, the two lieutenants among them. Colonel M. replied. He demanded punishment for the stationmaster, so negligent in his duties that he had shown himself incapable of reading correctly a number on a uniform collar. Moreover, the col-

21 juillet

départ de Malais, comme volontaire,
voyage j. ou 24 au matin par Angers
où je couche à l'hôtel et breakfast chez
les Louasse, St Pierre des Corps, Varzin,
le Creusot (Chau les cheminées fumantes
entre de hautes collines, — où nous nous
réveillons avec surprise le 23 au matin) Le
24 au matin nous nous réveillons en
Islette, — gare entre des collines boisées
que sous la haute lumière d'un matin
gris ressemble à un gare de Jura, à l'aube
d'un matin de vacances.

24 à une court marche nous mène au
cant. dépôt, de Bellefontaine, — très
agréable coin, à l'endroit de l'Argonne
où j'ai même eu l'impression de la
profonde forêt.

Last two pages of Bloch's journal: June–July 1915: return to the front

23 – les officiers et adjudants du conseil vont aux toilettes se faire ... affectés, – Je suis attribué à la 4e Cie

25 au 1er juillet. séjour aux toilettes, à la verrerie. Un peu d'exercice mais presque rien à faire; temps assez beau.

2e juillet au 7 juillet –

onel enclosed a copy of his report of the heroic deaths of the two lieutenants, adding that reading this document could hardly fail to inspire in the stationmaster the strength necessary to carry his so onerous duties to completion and to surmount all discouaragement. I can guarantee the truth of this anecdote. I learned it from a reliable source. Colonel M.'s command post was then at Bois-Aiguille. We were nearby and under his orders. I have never known the name of the stationmaster. Was he the one at Is-sur-Tille? I should like to think so. If not, it was his brother.

One thing gave our long trip a certain charm: the uncertainty of where we were in relation to what our objective should turn out to be. We knew that the 72d had left the region of Verdun, where it had just been in action. But where should we find it? Alsace? Artois? The Dardanelles? For myself, I asked nothing but to see more of the country. I had spent four months in the Argonne. I wanted a change.

On the morning of June 25, I awoke in a station where the coaches carrying our contingent had been left on a siding by the train to which they had been attached. The morning was brisk, the sky overcast. I could see a small station, a village, some meadows, and, shutting in the horizon on all sides, round hills covered with tall trees. This pleasant countryside, looking a bit gloomy in the gray light, reminded me of mountain regions I had known, and especially of the Jura. It seemed as if I had just left for vacation and was getting off at Vallorbe for a customs inspection. It was Les Islettes; it was the Argonne, where the regiment, reassigned to the Fifth Army Corps, had again been stationed, and where this time I would spend more than a year.

First we were sent to Bellefontaine, where the division depot was located. We spent a day and a night in this charming hamlet, which, at the bottom of its valley where the road stopped, isolated and surrounded by the forest, seemed as lost as if it were at the end of the earth. On June 26 I rejoined the regiment along with the officers and adjutants of the reinforcement unit. We left the men behind at the division depot. The 72d was, for the most part, quartered at Les Islettes. We reported to the colonel's office, and everyone received his assignment. As for me, I was attached to the fourth company, which was housed just beyond the village in a glassworks. That afternoon I assumed my duties as company adjutant and platoon leader.

I retain pleasant memories of Les Islettes, where this time I remained for five full days and where, as we shall see, I was to return again. One should envisage a rather large town, clean and comfortable, stretching along the Paris–Verdun road, set in meadows in the middle of the woods, its houses and barns bursting with troops. We were safe. The enemy had not yet installed the long-range artillery that at the time of the Verdun offensive would allow him to bombard the station and the village itself. We heard the cannon, but we did not fear the shells.

Here the manuscript of Marc Bloch ends.

BIBLIOGRAPHY

The life and work of Marc Bloch

Altman, Georges. "Au temps de la clandestinité: Notre 'Narbonne' de la Résistance." *Annales d'histoire sociale,* 1945, pp. 11–14.

Boutruche, Robert. "Marc Bloch vu par ses élèves." Publications de la Faculté des Lettres de l'Université de Strasbourg, *Memorial des années 1939–1945.* Paris: Belles Lettres, 1947.

Brâtianu, G. I. "Un savant et un soldat: Marc Bloch (1886–1944)." *Revue historique du sud-est européen* 23 (1946): 5–20.

Braudel, Fernand. "Marc Bloch." *International Encyclopedia of the Social Sciences,* vol. 2. New York: Macmillan, 1968.

Davies, R. R. "Marc Bloch." *History* 52, no. 176 (1967): 265–82.

Dollinger, Philippe. "Notre maître Marc Bloch: L'historien et sa méthode." *Revue d'histoire économique et sociale* 27 (1948–49): 109–26.

Febvre, Lucien. "Marc Bloch." In *Architects and Craftsmen in History: Festschrift für Abbott Payson Usher,* ed. Joseph T. Lambie. Tübingen: Mohr, 1956.

———. "Marc Bloch: Dix ans après." *Annales: Économies, sociétés, civilisations* 9, no. 2 (1954): 1–3.

———. "Marc Bloch et Strasbourg: Souvenirs d'une grande histoire." Publications de la Faculté des Lettres de l'Université de Strasbourg, *Memorial des années 1939–1945*. Paris: Belles Lettres, 1947. This article was reprinted in a slightly altered form in Febvre's *Combats pour histoire*. Paris: Armand Colin, 1953.

———. "Marc Bloch, 1886–1944." *Annales d'histoire sociale*, 1945, pp. 1–10.

———. "Marc Bloch: Témoignages sur la période 1939–1940. Extraits d'une correspondance intime." *Annales d'histoire sociale*, 1945, pp. 15–33.

Gilbert, Felix. "Three Twentieth-Century Historians: Meinecke, Bloch, Chabod." In *History: The Development of Historical Studies in the United States*, by John Higham, with Leonard Krieger and Felix Gilbert. Englewood Cliffs, N.J.: Prentice-Hall, 1965.

Ginsburg, Carlo. "A proposita della raccolta dei saggi storici di Marc Bloch." *Studi medievali*, 3 ser., 6 (1965): 335–53.

Hughes, H. Stuart. "The Historians and the Social Order." In *The Obstructed Path: French Social Thought in the Years of Desperation, 1930–1960*. New York: Harper & Row, 1966.

Larner, John. "Marc Bloch and *The Historian's Craft*." *Philosophical Journal* 2 (1965): 123–32.

Perrin, Charles-Edmond. "L'oeuvre historique de Marc Bloch." *Revue historique* 199, no 2 (1948): 161–88.

Raftis, J. Ambrose. "Marc Bloch's Comparative Method and the Rural History of Medieval England." *Medieval Studies* 24 (1962): 349–65.

Rhodes, R. Colbert. "Émile Durkheim and the Historical Thought of Marc Bloch." *Theory and Society* 6, no. 1 (1978): 45–73.

Sewell, William H., Jr. "Marc Bloch and the Logic of Comparative History." *History and Theory* 7 (1967): 208–18.

Stengers, J. "Marc Bloch et l'histoire." *Annales: Économies, sociétés, civilisations* 8 (1953): 329–37.

Bibliography

Walker, Lawrence. "Marc Bloch's *Feudal Society.*" *History and Theory* 3 (1963): 245–55.

Background materials

Aymard, Maurice. "The *Annales* and French Historiography." *Journal of Economic History* 1 (1972): 491–511.

Duby, Georges. "Histoire des mentalités." In *L'histoire et ses méthodes*, ed. Charles M. D. Samarin. Paris: Gallimard, 1961.

Glenisson, Jean. "L'historiographie française contemporaine: Tendances et réalisations." In *La recherche historique en France de 1940 à 1945*, issued by the Comité Française des Sciences Historiques. Paris: Centre National de la Recherche Scientifique, 1965.

Iggers, Georg. *New Directions in European Historiography.* Middletown, Conn.: Wesleyan University Press, 1975.

Keylor, William. *Academy and Community: The Foundation of the French Historical Profession.* Cambridge: Harvard University Press, 1975.

Marrou, Henri Irenée. *De la connaissance historique.* Paris: Editions du Seuil, 1964.

Siegel, Martin. "Science and the Historical Imagination in French Historiographical Thought, 1866–1914." Ph.D. dissertation, Columbia University, 1965.

Smith, Robert. "L'atmosphère politique à l'École Normale Supérieure à la fin du XIXe siècle." *Revue d'histoire moderne et contemporaine* 20 (1973): 248–69.

Stoianovich, Traian. *French Historical Method: The Annales Paradigm.* Ithaca, N.Y.: Cornell University Press, 1976.

Tint, Herbert. *The Decline of French Patriotism, 1870–1940.* London: Weidenfeld & Nicolson, 1964.

Weber, Eugen. *The Nationalist Revival in France, 1905–1914.* Berkeley: University of California Press, 1959.

MEMOIRS OF WAR, 1914–15

Designed by Richard E. Rosenbaum.
Composed by The Composing Room of Michigan, Inc.
in 11 point Palatino V.I.P., 3 points leaded,
with display lines in Palatino.
Printed offset by Vail-Ballou Press, Inc. on
Warren's Olde Style, 60 pound basis.
Bound by Vail-Ballou Press
in Joanna book cloth.

Library of Congress Cataloging in Publication Data

Bloch, Marc Léopold Benjamin, 1886–1944.
  Memoirs of war, 1914–15.

  Translation of Souvenirs de guerre, 1914–15.
  Bibliography: p.
  1. European War, 1914–1918—Personal narratives,
French.   2. Bloch, Marc Léopold Benjamin, 1886–1944.   I. Title.
D640.B581713   940.4'81'44   79-6849
ISBN 0-8014-1220-X